the jd jungle

LAW SCHOOL
SURVIVAL
GUIDE

the ᴶᵈjungle

LAW SCHOOL
SURVIVAL
GUIDE

From the Editors of *JD Jungle* and
jdjungle.com, the leading sources
of information for lawyers and law students

PERSEUS PUBLISHING
A MEMBER OF THE PERSEUS BOOKS GROUP

Cataloging-in-Publication Data is available from the Library of Congress
ISBN 0–7382–0749–7

Perseus Publishing is a Member of the Perseus Books Group.
Find us on the World Wide Web at http://www.perseuspublishing.com

Perseus Publishing books are available at special discounts for bulk purchases in the U.S. by corporations, institutions, and other organizations. For more information, please contact the Special Markets Department at the Perseus Books Group, 11 Cambridge Center, Cambridge, MA 02142, or call (800) 255–1514 or (617) 252–5298, or e-mail j.mccrary@perseusbooks.com.

Text design by Jeffrey P. Williams
Set in 11-point Janson Text by the Perseus Books Group

First printing, March 2003
1 2 3 4 5 6 7 8 9 10—06 05 04 03

contents

7 The Second Year: Land a Job   73

8 The Third Year: Relax   117

9 Behind the Bar   121

10 Inspiration   145

Introduction:
The Life of the Law

....

NO MATTER WHERE YOU GO, YOU CAN'T GET AWAY FROM THE LAW. THE LAW AFFECTS NATIONAL SECURITY (TERRORISM), PERSONAL SAFETY (GUN CONTROL), POLITICS (*BUSH* V. *GORE*), BUSINESS (ENRON), SCIENCE (cloning), entertainment (Napster), pop culture (*Judge Judy*), and just about anything else you can name.

A law degree is your ticket to the world of law. Without going to law school, it's nearly impossible to become a lawyer. And if you're not a lawyer, your ability to shape the law just isn't the same.

Why be a lawyer? For some, it's the satisfaction of locking up bad guys. For others, it's facilitating a $1 billion business deal. For still others, it's protecting the innocent, wiggling through a loophole in the tax code, or redefining the concept of intellectual property. (Of course, it doesn't hurt that the median base salary for first-year law firm associates was $95,000 in 2001.)

There's just one catch. Law school is hard. Very hard. And it's also expensive. Shirt-off-your-back expensive.

That's where this book comes in. The *JD Jungle Law School Survival Guide* will show you how to successfully navigate all three years of the law school experience. It will help you get accepted at the law school of your choice, find financial aid, study and take exams more effectively, manage stress, pass the bar exam, and land the job of your dreams.

The law is about power. It's about making a difference. It's about success. The *JD Jungle Law School Survival Guide* will help you achieve all three.

Jon Gluck
Editor, *JD Jungle*

Suma CM
Editor, jdjungle.com

Why Law School?

....

- Where Can a JD Take You?
- Will You Thrive?
- Do You Need a JD?
- Go for It

IF YOU'RE THINKING ABOUT LAW SCHOOL, YOU'RE NOT ALONE. AC-CORDING TO THE LAW SCHOOL ADMISSION COUNCIL (LSAC), 77,200 AMERICAN MEN AND WOMEN APPLIED FOR A JD IN 2001, AND THEIR reasons for doing so were probably just as numerous. Some may have envisioned fighting for justice; others, just fighting off financial insecurity with a fat paycheck. No matter what your reasons for considering law school, making the right decision requires careful consideration and self-examination.

Legal education has a lot of great things going for it, but it's certainly no cakewalk. Programs can be intense, time-consuming, and fiercely competitive (just ask any student in the thick of her first year). They're also expensive—tuition costs range from about $10,000 a year at a state school to almost $30,000 at a private institution, so by graduation time many aspiring lawyers are saddled with big debts. In addition, the curriculum takes at least three years to complete—longer if you're going part-time.

Here's what to consider before leaping into the world of law school.

WHERE CAN A JD TAKE YOU?

"The biggest misconception that parents and students have is that all lawyers put on a tie, go out, and deliver arguments in a courtroom," says Joyce Whittington, director of career services at the University of Mississippi School of Law. While there are definitely a few Ally McBeals, Matlocks, and JAGs running around the world, a law degree offers many options beyond cross-examining witnesses all day. Almost every institution and organization needs a lawyer at one time or another.

The typical graduate can choose from an array of careers, from major corporate law firm work to public-interest advocacy. Private law firms, the most common place for graduates to land, do everything from litigation work to tax law, real estate law, intellectual property, and government lobbying and regulation. Banks, consulting firms, and corporations employ JDs both as associates and as in-house counsel. A JD may also come in handy if someday you want to cut through all the red tape associated with starting your own business.

Whittington advises roughly 500 Mississippi law school students each year, helping them land summer internships, associate positions at firms, and clerkships with judges. Over the years, she's also placed JDs in less conventional careers, such as journalism, foreign service, and finance. "You can use your law degree for anything," she says, especially because it teaches you to write persuasively and to perform quick analysis.

WILL YOU THRIVE IN LAW SCHOOL?

How do you know if you're up for the career? Whittington advises prospective students to read as much as they can about the field.

Perhaps the best way to figure out if a JD is right for you is to spend a day pretending you're a law student. A little investigative research can go a long way. "Sit in on law school classes, talk to law students, and meet with faculty members," advises Andrew Leipold, associate dean at the University of Illinois College of Law, in Champaign.

Also consider the daily grind: You'll have to do homework, meet with study groups, and take exams all over again. The detail-oriented nature of legal education means that students are forced to read massive textbooks and assimilate information quickly. Logical reasoning is stressed, and law students are often required to think on their feet as they are subjected to professors' cold calls, heated classroom debates, and moot court competitions.

Barra Little, a Harvard Law School graduate who has advised more than 90 prelaw undergraduates, cautions that you have to be in the right frame of mind: "Think of what you'll be doing—analyzing short writing pieces, studying arguments and logic, doing clinicals (all for a grade)—and decide whether all of this appeals to you."

That's what Hilary Abell did before law school: After teaching kindergarten for a year, she was pretty sure she wanted to become a children's rights advocate. But first, she enrolled in an introduction to law class at Harvard's Extension School. "I wanted to be 150 percent certain that this was what I wanted to do," she says.

DO YOU REALLY NEED A JD?

JDs work in a variety of fields, and many of them pursue non-traditional careers after law school. Some go through the three-year program only to decide that they don't actually want to practice law.

After graduating from Georgetown University Law Center, David Flyer set up his own litigation practice in Washington, D.C. It didn't take long for him to realize that being a "traditional" lawyer wasn't for him. "I got tired of tearing things down and fighting with people," he says. "I wanted to build things up and shake hands." Flyer decided it was time for a career change and became the general manager (and general counsel) for Viaduct, an Internet professional services company; he's now the COO and general counsel for High-wheel Design Group, a web-development consulting firm.

Flyer has mixed feelings about his law degree. While he didn't enjoy his prior work as a lawyer, he's found the degree invaluable in his new career. A JD not only impressed re-cruiters but also gave him valuable skills. "You can definitely go out and do equally compelling work without a JD," he says. "But law school gives you knowledge and perspective that make you better at almost anything you'll do."

GO FOR IT

In the end, a law degree is what you make of it. "If you enjoy the world of ideas, then don't worry about whether you want to be a practicing lawyer, or whether you want to go into pol-itics or business or not-for-profit work," says Leipold. "Ask what makes you happy. And if you like the idea of law school and it feels right, then go for it."

Choosing the Right Law School

....

- Do Your Research
- Law School Specialties
- Dual Degrees
- Law School Later in Life

OKAY. YOU'VE SPENT MANY SLEEPLESS NIGHTS PONDERING THE LAST CHAPTER, CREATING PRO-AND-CON LISTS, CONSULTING COUNSELORS, AND ENGAGING IN SOME SERIOUS SOUL-SEARCHING. YOUR DECISION? Yes, law school is for you.

You know that a legal education teaches students how to acquire and analyze information, solve problems, and effectively articulate ideas. To successfully navigate the law school admissions process, follow these steps.

DO YOUR RESEARCH

The best way to begin the process is to contact your college's prelaw adviser. These gurus have the inside scoop on what schools are looking for in a candidate—and the information you need to increase your chances of getting in. They can help you assess your candidacy with a critical eye, provide you with the resources you need, and assist you in making an educated decision about where to apply.

Though it may be tempting to select schools by throwing darts at a rankings list, we suggest you take a more calculated approach and consider the following factors before making your choice:

Selectivity

Check out the schools' websites and compare your GPA and Law School Admission Test (LSAT) scores to those of students enrolled at the schools you're thinking about. James Bowers, a former admissions officer at Duke University School of Law, advises students to apply to a range of schools: "schools you're pretty darn certain you'll get into, schools where your scores are at the median, and of course the 'reaches.'"

Find out what individual programs are looking for in a candidate, then identify ways not only to meet those standards but also to differentiate yourself from your peers. Bill Hoye, associate dean of admissions at the University of Southern California Law School, says that the admissions process has become much more difficult because of the substantial increase in competitive candidates with excellent credentials. (Some schools have seen application numbers go up as much as 15–30 percent in recent years.) "We find ourselves denying applicants who in previous years may have been more competitive," Hoye says. With application rates soaring, it's critical that you stand out from the pack.

Geography

"Students do their best work where they are happiest," says Hoye. Whether you yearn to take a bite out of the Big Apple or to spend your study breaks in Malibu, there is a law school out there for you. While you don't *have* to attend school in the area where you intend to practice, admissions officers do encourage students to take full advantage of the opportunity to network locally. Many regional law firms don't go too far to recruit—they get all the associates they need at local schools, so you may be at a disadvantage if you're too far away.

Areas of Concentration

What type of law would you like to specialize in? Many schools have distinct strengths in certain curriculum areas. Find out who does what best. Cruise through schools' websites to see what they emphasize about curricula.

Fit

Check the schools' websites, talk to current and former students, and visit campuses if possible to see where you'll feel comfortable.

> TIP: Even if you're several years out of college, you may be able to use your alma mater's advising and career services offices (though some charge a fee).

LAW SCHOOL SPECIALTIES

Here are some schools to consider if you're interested in particular practice areas (source: *U.S. News & World Report*):

Clinical Training
Georgetown, New York University, American University (Washington, D.C.), CUNY–Queens College, Yale.

Tax Law
NYU, University of Florida (Levin), Georgetown, Harvard, Yale.

Trial Advocacy
Stetson, Temple (Beasley), Georgetown, Northwestern, Samford (Cumberland).

International Law
NYU, Columbia, Harvard, Georgetown, Yale.

Health Care Law
University of Houston, Boston University, Loyola University Chicago, St. Louis University, University of Maryland.

Environmental Law
Lewis and Clark's Northwestern School, Vermont Law School, Pace, Stanford, University of Maryland.

Dispute Resolution
Harvard, Pepperdine, Ohio State, University of Missouri–Columbia, Hamline.

Intellectual Property Law
UC-Berkeley (Boalt Hall), George Washington, Franklin Pierce Law Center, NYU, Yeshiva University (Cardozo), University of Houston.

DUAL DEGREES

What if you're interested in pursuing two degrees simultaneously? Many schools allow you to pair the JD with an MD, an MBA, or another program.

Kim Doody has based her future on a combination of her three favorite TV shows—*ER*, *Law & Order*, and *The West Wing*. Though she wants to practice medicine as a forensic psychiatrist, she also has her sights set on eventually becoming a health policy expert, drafting legislation and steering the nation's health care agenda. In a nutshell, she's aiming to be a future surgeon general or secretary of Health and Human Services. "I want to be in a place where I can effect changes in health policy," she says.

But Doody knew she needed to do more than just immerse herself in NBC's prime-time lineup. So she enrolled in a joint-degree program at Southern Illinois University that allows her to simultaneously earn a JD and an MD.

Dancing this graduate degree two-step certainly isn't for everyone, but Doody says that obtaining the extra law degree will make all the difference in reaching her career goal. "I feel like I could go in and write law right now. I can understand legislation," she says.

Although students enrolled in joint-degree programs make up only about 10 percent of the JD student population, many like Doody have decided that two degrees are better than one. And schools across the country have made joint degrees easier than ever to obtain by combining programs that attract students with all types of interests. Law students, for example, can get additional degrees in business, social work, public policy, international studies, computer science—even religion.

For those with a focus like Doody's, dual degrees offer the opportunity to specialize by combining two disciplines that will help them reach their career goals. "I think that for students with particular interests, a [dual-degree] program has special value," said Eugene Basanta, a law professor at Southern Illinois University who codirects the school's JD-MD program.

Less Time, More Skills

Joint-degree programs also give students the chance to reduce the amount of time it ordinarily takes to get graduate degrees. For instance, a JD-MBA usually takes only four years (five semesters of law school and three of B-school)—one fewer semester for each discipline. A JD-MD takes six years instead of the usual seven it would take to earn the degrees back to back. Obtaining a joint degree can also be cheaper than getting degrees separately. A JD-MBA at Northwestern, for example, costs roughly $104,000—a savings of almost $47,000.

The skills and knowledge that come with a dual degree can provide a competitive edge in a tough job market. In the early

1990s, Karl Schieneman was enrolled in the MBA program at Carnegie Mellon's Graduate School of Industrial Administration. But he feared that in such a poor economy, an MBA alone might not land him the job of his dreams. So he decided to get a law degree, which Carnegie Mellon and the University of Pittsburgh offer in a joint program, to bolster his resumé.

After graduation, he worked as an accountant but later switched gears to work as a temp attorney for a large Pittsburgh law firm, a job that inspired his current business. In 1995, he started Legal Network Ltd., a Pittsburgh-based placement service for temporary and contract attorneys. Schieneman, now in his late thirties, gives much of the credit for his success to his two degrees. "The MBA has been very helpful," he says. "I have been able to use my business background to analyze law firm operations . . . and how we can help make them better legal organizations."

Worthwhile, or Wasted Effort?

The jury's still out on whether two degrees always make sense, particularly for those set on practicing law. For starters, recruiters from big law firms sometimes look down on applicants with joint degrees. Anne Brandt, associate director of the Law School Admission Council, explains that these firms not only shell out big bucks for their young associate hires but also spend a lot of time training them. As a result, she says, some firms are wary of any hint—such as a second degree— that might indicate a lack of commitment to practicing law.

Geoffrey Lee, president of Counsel Source, an attorney recruiting firm in Dallas, adds that students intent on practicing law after graduation should focus on improving their class rank rather than chasing down a second degree. From the perspective of a big firm, he argues, having knockout grades beats having two degrees, especially if the grades in both disciplines are mediocre.

In addition, Brandt points out that you don't always need a second degree to specialize in a particular area of the law. She says that most top law schools offer a wide array of courses for students who want to concentrate on subjects off the beaten path. "It is not necessary to have a degree in computer science to represent a dot-com," she says.

Expensive—and Tough

Another downside to dual degrees is the sheer expense. The cost of a four-year JD-MBA at the University of Pennsylvania, for example, is roughly $160,000 for room, board, and tuition, whereas a JD alone costs $117,201. "You're amassing an amazing amount of debt," says Rose Martinelli, director of MBA admissions and financial aid at Penn's Wharton School. "You have to be silly to get a degree that you're not going to use."

A joint program isn't only hard on your wallet. It's also stressful and time-consuming. "There are going to be some dark days and long nights," says Southern Illinois University's Basanta. "You need to have the emotional, intellectual, and physical commitment."

GOING TO LAW
SCHOOL LATER IN LIFE

The typical law school student is between the ages of 23 and 26, but according to the LSAC 21.8 percent of all law school applicants in 1999–2000 were over 30. Though their reasons for seeking a legal education and their experiences in their programs vary, the consensus remains: School isn't just for "kids."

Many JD programs have flexible schedules that accommodate older students. In addition to offering a full-time program with daytime courses, schools offer evening classes and part-time curricula, allowing students to graduate in anywhere from three to six years. This range of options is allowing more and more midlifers to pursue law degrees.

Why They Go and What They Do

Unlike some of their younger counterparts, mature JDs tend to have specific career goals in mind when enrolling in law school. Everett Bellamy, an assistant dean at Georgetown Law Center, believes there are several motivational factors: Some seek to strengthen their skills within their chosen industry; others are looking to make a career switch; and still others go simply for the intellectual stimulation.

Building on Experience

Lucille Roussin already held a Ph.D. and taught art history and archaeology at Sarah Lawrence College in Bronxville, New York, and Cooper Union in New York City, before she decided to enroll in the full-time program at New York's Benjamin N. Cardozo School of Law. Over the years she'd become interested in stolen artwork and antiquities and wanted to help governments reclaim their cultural treasures. After consulting with friends and colleagues, she decided to take the plunge and apply to law school at age 49. "The whole thing was bizarre," she says. "Suddenly I was on the other side of the podium, taking the Princeton Review LSAT-prep course with a bunch of 20-year-olds and starting my first year at school all over again." Today, Roussin is an adjunct professor at Cardozo and has a thriving private practice specializing in Holocaust restitution claims.

Developing New Skills

Like their younger classmates, some older JDs are just beginning their professional careers. Margaret Utterback worked as a naval officer right after college but had been a stay-at-home mom for 10 years when she applied to the University of Wisconsin Law School in Madison. "I was lacking intellectual stimulation," she explains. "Once my kids started going to school full-time, I wanted to get my brain back in the groove." Utterback, now in her late thirties, was president of Wisconsin's student support group, OWLS (Older Wiser Law Students), and is now an associate at Madison's Quarles & Brady.

Expanding Your Mind

Walter Pincus covered national security issues at the *Washington Post* for almost 40 years; at 68, he donned his cap and gown at Georgetown Law's graduation. For Pincus, the decision to enroll in the part-time program was motivated by his desire to take on a new challenge. He continues to write for the *Post*, whose editors were supportive of his "extracurricular" activity. "The experience has been terrific," says Pincus. "And," he adds, "I was older than most of my professors."

The Upside

Law school faculty have welcomed older students. Georgetown's Bellamy says that though older JDs are held to the same competitive admissions criteria as the twentysomething crowd, Georgetown considers the breadth of life experience when reviewing older applicants. So, while your LSATs need to be high, job performance matters far more than, say, how many extracurriculars you pursued in college 15 years ago.

Gregory Ogden, who teaches civil procedure and administrative law at Pepperdine, believes that older students enhance class discussions. "They bring a perspective and maturity that help us deal with conflicts and problems," he says. As faculty adviser to several of the school's law journals, he believes that the over-30 JDs prove stronger in work-related skills such as cooperation and management. "They have a stabilizing influence on group projects," he points out. Wisconsin's assistant dean for student and academic affairs, Ruth Robarts, who went to law school after working as a high school principal for 10 years, agrees. She believes that her prior experience made her a better student. "You're just more focused and more mature," she says.

The Challenges

There are some drawbacks to heading to law school later in life. Older JDs don't always enjoy the same opportunities as their younger counterparts. Lucrative partner-track jobs at firms often demand young blood—eager recruits with a minimum of outside commitments who can log insane hours as associates. Adnan Latis, a thirtysomething law student at Wisconsin, acknowledges, "There is a stigma. I would be in a better position at a firm if I were younger, because they expect you to work 100 hours a week." With a wife and two children, Latis is unable to make that kind of commitment. However, he notes that older students can find niches within the legal field. Firms will often create more reasonable schedules for older associates with useful experience. Corporations and not-for-profits also readily hire older graduates as in-house counsel.

Another hurdle older students face is readjusting to the rigors of school. "I wasn't used to studying anymore," says Roussin. "I had to discipline myself again." But with time, Roussin found that she was able to develop an effective studying strategy, devoting blocks of time to reviewing at home, and she succeeded.

Latis, who moved his wife and two children from Nevada to study in Madison, has no regrets about his decision. "If you really want to do something, don't ever make age a hindrance to your objectives," he says. "It's just an excuse."

Paying for Your Education

....

- Loans
- Scholarships
- Work
- Loan Forgiveness

NO MATTER HOW AND WHEN YOU GO TO LAW SCHOOL, THE OLD ADAGE HOLDS TRUE: YOU HAVE TO SPEND MONEY TO MAKE MONEY. BECOMING A LAWYER IS NO EXCEPTION—YOU MAY ANTICIPATE EARNING SIX figures as an attorney, but law school expenses can set you back more than $130,000. So before you trot into Excellence & Wealth LLC decked out in Armani, you need to figure out how to pay for your education.

LOANS

Although scholarships, grants, and good old-fashioned employment are all available to help finance a JD, most students take on loans. According to the Law School Admission Council, approximately 80 percent of law students borrow at least some money to cover tuition, books, an apartment, and a steady supply of macaroni and cheese. Loan money comes from three major sources: individual law schools, the federal government, and private lending companies. The size of packages available, as well as differences in payback plans and interest rates, will help determine which source—or combination of sources—is best for you. Students who borrow from federal and private sources graduate with an average debt of $80,000; those with only government loans generally owe about $61,000, according to the LSAC.

Aid from Schools

Most students first hit up the financial aid office of the school they choose. Schools generally offer money more freely and with fewer contingencies than other lenders, because the aid is not always closely tied to need. Many, including Temple University's Beasley School of Law, do not require students to include parental income information when they apply for scholarships, grants, and loans. Some schools even dish out "emergency loans" if you're suddenly short on cash in the midst of your three years. Washburn University School of Law, in Kansas, administers federal aid programs through the university's financial aid office; but the law school has its own stash of funding to help students (usually those who have already applied for federal financial aid) with short-term emergency loans. Similarly, Tulane Law School, in New Orleans, and the Northwestern School of Law of Lewis & Clark College, in Oregon, maintain specific funds for emergency loans.

The flip side to borrowing money from schools is that they may ask you to pay it back more quickly than the government or a private lender would. They may also allow you to borrow more money than you need. That can be dangerous. The more cash you request today, the more you will have to pay back—with interest. And you shouldn't have to subsist on ramen noodles *after* law school.

Government Loans

You will probably take out private as well as government loans, but check with the public sources first. Federal loans such as unsubsidized or subsidized Stafford Loans (the latter are based on need and don't accrue interest while you're in school) offer the lowest interest rates and do not require a credit check. You merely have to fill out the Free Application for Federal Student Aid (FAFSA). And people are definitely taking advantage of Uncle Sam's help: In fiscal year 2000, some 8.4 million undergraduate and graduate students borrowed $51.4 billion from the federal government, according to Joe Aiello, media relations director of the government's Student Financial Assistance department. You must apply to renew federal loans every year by filing a new FAFSA, and your loan eligibility is subject to change during your school term (say, due to inheritance or marriage).

Private Loans

You might not qualify for all forms of federal aid (for example, your spouse may earn too much). But if Daddy Warbucks isn't writing your tuition checks, a private loan organization can help you finance your education.

"Different people are comfortable with different amounts of debt," says Pat Curry, communications director at Access Group, Inc., a major nonprofit private lending organization. "The biggest thing is really just planning and researching and being prepared." Curry stresses that groundwork must include ensuring your eligibility: Pay off all debts and credit cards before applying for private loans, which rely on credit checks for students and/or their cosigners.

Sallie Mae, the largest private provider of educational funding in the United States, offers a LAWLOANS program in conjunction with other lenders. To qualify for its private loan, you must request a Federal Stafford Loan first, but you can apply for both from its website or call 800–984–0190. A Sallie Mae representative says that many entering law students have already reached the maximum federal aid allowance while financing their undergraduate educations. For them, private loans are available—with a benefit come graduation time: "You always want to use your law study loans, because then you are eligible for a bar study loan [when you are studying for the bar exam]."

Sallie Mae's annual loans stretch from $500 to the maximum education cost a student faces (minus other aid received) and have a nine-month postgraduation grace period before repayment begins. Interest rates and fees vary depending on where you attend school and whether you enlist a coborrower but may be as low as $50 per month. Graduates may elect to pay only the interest for two to four years after they earn the diploma. Furthermore, if you need to drop out for a semester before the loan is fully disbursed, you are eligible to apply for new loans as soon as the law school returns the money. And if you become permanently disabled, the government steps in and picks up the tab.

SCHOLARSHIPS

If the mere thought of taking on debt induces an anxiety attack, there are a few ways to avoid it and still sport "Esq." after your name.

Jennifer, a student at Saint John's University School of Law, in New York, got three fat envelopes from admissions offices—and three fat envelopes from financial aid offices. While both Catholic University of America's Columbus School of Law and Penn State University offered her partial tuition packages, St. John's offered her a free ride. Jennifer had a tough time making her decision, though, since Catholic had offered her a spot in its prestigious communications law program. But a dean at Catholic admitted that leaving law school without loans would provide Jennifer with more freedom to pursue her career path of choice without financial obligations clouding her decisions. "He basically told me, 'Holy cow! Take it!'" Jennifer says. And she did, opting to go with the full academic scholarship. It has certainly paid off: Though many first-year law students (1Ls) feel the heat when their only summer job offers are for unpaid positions, the money Jennifer saved on tuition allowed her to seek—and accept—a summer internship in the public sector.

Many schools offer need-blind merit scholarships, as well as grants to cover demonstrated need. For example, the University of Dayton School of Law, in Ohio, awarded scholarships (ranging from $2,500 to full tuition) to at least 90 of the 167 members of its fall 1999 incoming class. Dayton is one of many law schools that dole out scholarships based on information included on applications for admission: LSAT scores, undergraduate GPAs, and the like. Other schools require prospective students to file separate scholarship applications with their applications for admission. Prospective students at Drake University Law School, in Des Moines, Iowa, for example, are considered for the Dwight D. Opperman full-tuition scholarship when they complete separate applications for admission and merit-based aid. The key to ensuring that you have the best chance to win that money is to apply as early as possible.

As with federal aid, be aware that a change in your financial status during your three-year stint can negate your eligibility. One veteran attorney got married the day after her first-year final exams at Harvard Law School. She returned from her honeymoon to find a letter from HLS congratulating her on her recent marriage—and revoking her scholarship since she was now part of a "family unit" with income.

WORK

The American Bar Association lets law students work only 20 hours per week while they're in school. Though the origins of that standard are "lost in history," it remains firm, says Barry Currier, the ABA deputy consultant on legal education. "The reason for the rule is pretty self-evident—law school is a serious enterprise and takes a substantial part of a person's energy and time. If you're going to be doing it full-time, you need to be doing it full-time."

Find a law student with more time than that, and you've found a superhero—or someone who needs an academic priority adjustment. "It's naïve for us in legal education not to think that students are under a good deal of [financial] pressure," Currier adds. "But it's also naive on the part of students to say, 'I'm going to work more and study less.'"

Still, for those willing to part with a few hours of precious study time, there are ample opportunities to temp or intern for pay. And some law school programs even feature part-time or flexible schedules for students who work during the day.

Career services offices are known for filling students' in-boxes with names of employers who need law students to lend helping hands. If you'd like extra cash, these notices can be saving graces. Whether you end up researching, helping in court, or doing errands, you'll probably make a decent hourly wage and learn a few tricks of the trade. There are also federal work-study programs (based on financial need) that allow students to earn money by working around campus—in computer labs and libraries, as tour guides, or as teaching assistants, for example. Some summer jobs also offer work-study money.

Finally, third-year law students with job offers in hand often work part-time for their future employers. One 3L at Georgetown University earned approximately $525 per week working at the firm where she would be an associate. A journal and a clinic kept her busy as a 2L, but her third-year course load of 14 credits left her with "plenty of time" to work at the firm and help her family's piggy bank grow.

LOAN FORGIVENESS

Law students who go on to work in the public-interest sector may benefit from loan-forgiveness programs. For example, in 1987 Northeastern University's School of Law—ranked number one in public-interest law by the ABA's student division—established the Fund for Public Interest to help do-gooders by deferring, lowering, and even forgiving their tuition expenses. Other schools are following suit: Ever since the National Association for Public Interest Law (now called Equal Justice Works) released an overview of loan repayment assistance options, the number of schools seeking to start or revamp their own programs has grown dramatically.

Uncle Sam may also lend a hand to the socially minded. Qualified grads willing to defer practicing law to participate in AmeriCorps may be eligible for education assistance.

RESOURCES

Free Application for Federal Student Aid:
www.fafsa.ed.gov

Access Group:
www.accessgroup.org
302–477–4190 or 800–282–1550

Sallie Mae LAWLOANS:
www.salliemae.com/apply/borrowing/lawloans.html
800–984–0190

Fleet:
www.fleet.com/education
888-FLEET-GO (888–353–3846)

TERI Alternative Loan:
www.teri.org
800–255–8374

Nellie Mae LawEXCEL:
www.nelliemae.com/loancenter/lawexcel_details.html
800–634–9308

Scholarships:
www.wiredscholar.com
www.fastweb.com

Making the Cut

- Acing the LSAT
- Transcripts
- Recommendations
- Personal Statement
- The Big Choice

YOU'VE NARROWED DOWN YOUR LIST OF SCHOOLS? GREAT. IT'S TIME TO APPLY. WHILE THE OPINIONS OF ADMISSIONS OFFICERS ARE USUALLY AS NUMEROUS AS THE APPLICATIONS THEY REVIEW, MOST AGREE on one thing: Apply early! There are countless others vying for a spot in next year's 1L class, so you don't want your personal statement on the virtues of a semester abroad in Oaxaca to be the nine-hundredth one that gets read. Admissions are rolling, but the latest date to submit your materials is usually in mid-March.

Virtually all law school applications have four parts: Law School Admission Test scores, undergraduate and graduate transcripts, three letters of recommendation, and a personal statement or writing sample. Most American Bar Association–accredited law schools require applicants to subscribe to the Law School Data Assembly Service (LSDAS), administered by the Law School Admission Council. The service prepares and provides schools with a report that includes all of your application materials and a summary of your undergraduate academic record.

If you are applying exclusively to law schools in Canada, you are not required to subscribe to the LSDAS. Some foreign-educated applicants may not be eligible for the LSDAS; check the website for details.

> **TIP:** Although you may feel that what you express on paper is but a glimpse of the depth of your character, don't wait for an interview to wow the admissions committee. Unlike other graduate programs, law schools rarely conduct interviews—so your application is your best chance to prove you belong there.

ACING THE LSAT

Ah, those dreaded four letters. Although opinions differ on the LSAT's accuracy in predicting how well a student will perform in law school, the test still carries tremendous weight. The LSAT and your undergraduate grades, in fact, are the two most important factors in any law school application. Law schools may accept a range of scores, but to remain competitive your score should probably be at or above the median at your school of choice.

Fortunately, you can prepare yourself for the exam by becoming better acquainted with it.

Why the LSAT?

The LSAT is a universal yardstick used to quantify the abilities that law schools are looking for in candidates who come from disparate academic backgrounds. According to Seppy Basili, the vice president of learning and assessment at Kaplan education centers, the LSAT is actually the most highly accurate predictor of a student's performance during the first year of law school. And the first year is the toughest nut to crack: If you can get through it, you will most likely succeed in your second and third years as well.

When to Take the Test

The LSAT is administered four times a year—on Saturday mornings in October, December, and February, and on a Monday afternoon in June. Alternate administrations are offered for Saturday Sabbath observers. The fee for the test is $103, and the deadline for registration generally falls one month before the test date.

In order to ensure that your scores are reported in time for fall admission, most of the 200 accredited law schools in the United States and Canada recommend that you take the LSAT by the December administration of the previous year. At the time of registration, you can elect to have your score report sent to one school for free; after that, there's a fee for each extra report.

Because your LSAT score is valid for only five years, you shouldn't take it too far in advance of when you plan to apply to schools.

TIP: If you're planning to apply shortly after you get your bachelor's degree, consider taking the LSAT during your senior year in college, while you're still in academic mode.

What's on the Test?

Here's the good news: There's no math. The LSAT is made up of five 35-minute multiple-choice sections: two logical reasoning, one logic games, one reading comprehension, and an experimental section that may contain any one of the above. The experimental section tests new questions for future LSAT-takers. Unless you're blessed with psychic powers, you won't know which one it is, so don't waste time trying to figure it out.

TIP: Because there is no penalty for a wrong answer on the LSAT, you should never leave a question blank. You may be able to garner a couple of extra points by making some educated guesses.

Here's a rundown of the three types of questions. Examples are taken from the October 1996 exam.

Logical reasoning (25 to 28 questions) is just what it sounds like: You are presented with a statement or an argument called a "stimulus," and your job is to answer questions based on the conclusions and inferences you draw from it. This tests your complex reasoning abilities, which will be integral to your success in law school. Logical reasoning is the most important type of question on the test, because your performance on these two sections accounts for roughly 50 percent of your total scaled score.

TIP: Remember, you must consider only the information you are given in the stimulus. The argument may be false, or you may disagree with it, but your job is just to identify its weaknesses. Don't make assumptions, and read each question very carefully.

Example:

Someone who gets sick from eating a meal will often develop a strong distaste for the one food in the meal that had the most distinctive flavor, whether or not that food caused the sickness. This phenomenon explains why children are especially likely to develop strong aversions to some foods.

Which one of the following, if true, provides the strongest support for the explanation?

(a) Children are more likely than adults to be given meals composed of foods lacking especially distinctive flavors.

(b) Children are less likely than adults to see a connection between their health and the foods they eat.

(c) Children tend to have more acute taste and to become sick more often than adults do.

(d) Children typically recover more slowly than adults do from sickness caused by food.

(e) Children are more likely than are adults to refuse to eat unfamiliar foods.

(Answer: C)

TIP: You have just 35 minutes to answer about 25 of these questions. Don't get bogged down on any one question—if you find yourself suffering over two answer choices, make your best guess and *let it go*. You've got a good shot if you can eliminate one or more wrong answers, and you're not going to be penalized if you don't get it right—only rewarded if you do. Once you've answered the question, put it out of your mind and move on to the next one.

Logic games or analytical reasoning (24 to 26 questions, usually four games) is the section that most often throws LSAT first-timers for a loop. Logic games test your ability to organize information in intricate relationships and then draw reasonable conclusions to answer questions. Although perhaps the most daunting, the logic games section is eminently coachable, and students tend to improve their logic games scores greatly with preparation and practice.

Example:
A jeweler makes a single strand of beads by threading onto a string in a single direction from a clasp a series of solid-colored beads. Each bead is either green, orange, purple, red, or yellow. The resulting strand satisfies the following specifications:

If a purple bead is adjacent to a yellow bead, any bead that immediately follows and any bead that immediately precedes that pair must be red.

Any pair of beads adjacent to each other that are the same color as each other must be green.

No orange bead can be adjacent to any red bead.

Any portion of the strand containing eight consecutive beads must include at least one bead of each color.

If the strand has exactly eight beads, which one of the following is an acceptable order, starting from the clasp, for the eight beads?

(a) Green, red, purple, yellow, red, orange, green, purple
(b) Orange, yellow, red, red, yellow, purple, red, green
(c) Purple, yellow, red, green, green, orange, yellow, orange
(d) Red, orange, red, yellow, purple, green, yellow, green
(e) Red, yellow, purple, red, green, red, green, green

(Answer: C)

> **TIP:** Because logic games are so coachable, LSAC has responded by creating increasingly more difficult games. In order to ensure that you're practicing logic games at the same level of difficulty that you'll encounter on test day, don't practice games from tests that are from the early 1990s—they're too easy.

Reading comprehension (25 to 28 questions, four passages of about 500 words) tests your ability to deconstruct an excerpted piece of text in order to answer questions about its main idea, tone, writing techniques, specific details, assumptions, and application to a hypothetical situation. Topics can range from the evolution of woodwind instruments to the mating rituals of monkeys in the rain forest. Questions could include:

• Which one of the following best states the main point of the passage?
• Which one of the following best describes the author's attitude?

- Which one of the following best describes the organization of the passage?

> TIP: Because these sections tend to be the most dense and difficult to get through, and because the questions are arranged by difficulty after each passage, browse all the passage topics first and then start with the one that interests you most. It's generally easier to focus on a topic that intrigues you, and if you run out of time and don't get to one of the passages in the section, it might as well be the most boring one.

At the end of the test, there is a 30-minute **writing sample** that presents you with a controversial issue and asks you to write an essay advocating a particular position. Though it's never graded, copies are sent along with your score reports to the schools. The personal statement on your application is much more important, though. One Washington, D.C., lawyer and LSAT expert says, "As long as you pick a side and answer the question, the writing sample shouldn't detract from your application. Don't waste too much time worrying about preparing for it, because it doesn't get factored into your LSAT score."

Example:

Roberto Martinez, owner of a small used bookstore, has recently purchased an adjacent store and is deciding how best to use it to expand his business. Write an argument in support of one plan over the other based on the following criteria:

- Martinez wants to attract a significant number of new customers.
- Martinez wants to retain the loyal clientele that looks to him for out-of-print books and first editions.

One plan is for Martinez to begin carrying best-sellers and popular fiction. Because of his downtown location, publishers of these works are likely to put his store on their book tours; although the large bookstore chains have taken hold in the suburbs, none have yet located in the downtown area. Under this plan, however, Martinez would have enough room to keep only the best books from his current inventory. To capitalize on this collection, he is considering an occasional evening series called "Rediscoveries," featuring discussions of authors whose out-of-print books he carries, particularly several authors who are currently enjoying a resurgence of critical attention.

An alternative plan is for Martinez to use the new space to open a small coffeehouse with a limited menu. He would furnish the area as a sitting room with couches and chairs and a few regular dining tables. Although there are several restaurants nearby, they offer primarily full meals in more formal settings. Retaining much of his inventory of used books, he would add novels, poetry, and nonfiction published by small presses to feature lesser-known writers whose work is difficult to find in this community. These small presses include a number of local authors who are eager to read and discuss their work in the coffeehouse.

TIP: Follow the directions. Don't come up with a third possible argument or get too creative with your answer. Also note that in their instructions, the LSAC states: "Law schools are interested in how skillfully you support the position you take and how clearly you express that position. How well you write is much more important than how much you write."

Your Score

The LSAT is scored on a scale of 120 to 180. Score ranges vary from school to school, so research your schools of interest to find out what their middle 50 percent ranges are.

Solid candidates for top-10 law schools typically score in the ninetieth percentile or higher. That means at least a 164.

But don't give up if your score is lower—these are only ranges, and an impressive essay and stellar GPA can sometimes make up for missed points on the LSAT.

You may take the LSAT up to three times in any two-year period, but be careful about taking the test too many times. LSAC reports not only your best or most recent score but also all other scores and test cancellations over the past five years. In addition, it will include a score average if you've taken more than one exam, plus a score band for each test you have taken. Score bands span from three points below to three points above your actual score and indicate the possibility for error in gauging your ability level. These bands are intended to discourage admissions officers from placing too much emphasis on minute score discrepancies between students.

Schools don't like to see too many test scores—it's indicative of a student who can't get his act together to prepare for a test and perform to the best of his ability. Of course, if you feel the score is a serious misrepresentation of your ability level, it is to your benefit to take the test again.

Hilary, a second-time test-taker, improved her score by five points. She attributes her initial performance to nerves and her unfamiliarity with the territory and exam-day situation. "I knew what I needed to do to make myself comfortable the second time," she says. She could visualize the test and see what was coming next. She was also familiar with the timing of each section so that she could pace herself accordingly.

TIP: If your score increases dramatically, you might want to address the original score abnormality—perhaps in an attachment to your personal statement (but not within the personal statement itself). Kaplan's Basili suggests having a recommendation writer drop a small explanation in his or her letter to the admissions office—for example, "I know that Nicole was having a difficult time coping with the loss of her grandfather at the time she was preparing to take her first LSAT."

To Prep or Not to Prep?

"Preparation has now become the standard," says Basili. "The cat's out of the bag. Test prep works." Not only does it familiarize you with the exam; it also reduces the stress associated with test-taking. According to Basili, "Confidence is a lot of the value that test prep provides." If you know you've done all you can to prepare for the exam, you can walk into the room on test day and feel secure. You'll know from your practice tests how well you've been doing and how much your score has increased; and even if you're scoring spot-on in the fiftieth percentile, you'll be able to look around the room and know that you're going to do as well as or better than half the people there.

Also, because the LSAT is still a paper-and-pencil test (unlike the GMAT and GRE, which are administered via computer), test-takers have the luxury of skipping around within a section, getting points where they can, and coming back to the more difficult questions later. Being familiar enough with the exam to have an attack strategy for each section is a security blanket: You'll know what kinds of questions to expect, which ones you're best at, and how to break up the section to maximize the number of questions you answer correctly.

How do you find a preparation method that best suits your needs? Start by taking a free practice test (the LSAC offers a downloadable version at www.lsac.org, and Kaplan will provide a paper-and-pencil version upon request). This exercise will show you where your strengths and weaknesses are and how many points you need to add to hit your target score.

Next, do a little preliminary self-assessment: Are you already an excellent test-taker, or do you have a specific weakness that needs to be addressed? If so, a private tutor may be right for you. Do you work better in a group setting and learn more easily when your peers ask questions and provide explanations? A prep course might be your best option. And—not to be overlooked—consider what you can afford.

> TIP: Don't bother taking a practice test online. Because it's such a different format, it won't predict your score as accurately as a paper-and-pencil exam will. If you download the LSAC's test, print it out before you take it.

The biggest and best names in LSAT prep are Kaplan and Princeton Review. They've earned their reputations by hiring highly qualified instructors, putting them through a rigorous training process, and consistently reviewing and updating their curricula. Kaplan, which reports an average score increase of 7.2 points, touts its commitment to teaching strategies, not just "tricks." Princeton Review hangs its hat on the fact that its classes are small and grouped by ability level, so you know you'll be in a class with people who learn at the same pace as you. Both groups charge about $1,000 for a course.

It's best to start preparing as far in advance of your test date as possible. Most courses accommodate students who plan ahead, offering course schedules that meet once a week for eight to ten weeks (sessions last for two to three hours) and run up until the test date. But these courses also make room for slackers and can still help you out if you have only a month or so before you want to take the exam—just be prepared to sacrifice more time per week.

> TIP: Ask about extra help sessions you might attend and office hours with instructors. Test-prep companies want you to succeed so that you'll tell your friends about your wonderful experience, and they're usually willing to go out of their way to help you achieve your goals.

If you have the funds, you may want to hire a private tutor. With personalized attention tailored to your ability level, you won't waste time going over sections you're already acing. You may also feel more comfortable asking questions and going over explanations until you get it right. Expect to pay between $100 and $200 an hour for a private tutor from Kaplan or Princeton Review, or between $50 and $100 for an independent instructor or graduate student.

At a minimum, order a few additional practice exams from the LSAC at www.lsac.org (they've published nearly all their exams since 1991), at $8 a pop. LSAC also publishes a book titled *10 Actual, Official LSAT PrepTests* for $30—definitely the thriftiest option. Remember that the tests have become harder over the years, so practice with tests that were administered within the past several years, saving two or three of the most recent tests for last.

TIP: Simulate the real testing atmosphere in at least a couple of your practice exams: Time yourself accurately; do all sections; take breaks where required; and be far away from phones, refrigerators, and the comforts of home.

Test Day Tips

The test day itself presents unique challenges. Here's how to do your best:

Take it easy the night before. A former Kaplan LSAT instructor suggests spending a little time reviewing what you've learned in order to reinforce confidence—but no hard-core studying. You need rest, and you need to be ready to go early in the morning.

Practice waking up and getting ready for an early test. Your body and mind will become accustomed to the hour.

Back up your wake-up. The last time you had to get out of bed this early on a Saturday was probably to watch *Superfriends*, so set two alarm clocks and get a friend to give you a wake-up call.

Make sure that on test day you're visiting your testing location for *at least* the second time. Practice driving there at the same time and day of the week so you'll know the route and the traffic patterns; know where you're going to park your car; visit the exam room; and find bathrooms and water fountains. If you notice any major problems with your testing site—for example, a hotel ballroom with dim lighting and no windows—voice your concerns to the LSAC immediately. Lisa, an LSAT-taker in Virginia, visited her testing site a few days before the exam only to find that they were repainting the building. Being extremely allergic to paint fumes, she notified LSAC officials, who were able to find a seat for her at another location in the area.

Dress comfortably and in layers. Exam rooms are notorious for temperamental thermostats.

Bring your registration forms, IDs, and an adequate supply of No. 2 pencils. Watches are permitted, but don't bring anything that beeps, including timers or cell phones. Such devices are not allowed, and even if the proctor doesn't catch it at the beginning, you'll make a lot of enemies when that Samba ring echoes through the test room.

Bring water and a high-energy snack for the break. Bring something like a banana or a protein bar that's not too messy, even if you don't think you'll need it. During the breaks, find a quiet space away from your fellow test-takers so that you won't get unnerved listening to their conversations.

No testing experience is perfect, so be prepared to roll with the punches. Proctors are sometimes late, desk space can be tiny, and someone in the back of the room will inevitably have a head cold or a foot-tapping tic. Block out external distractions and focus on the task at hand.

You have five days after the test to cancel your score, so even if you think you did horribly, *wait* before making that decision. You should only cancel if there were test-day factors that seriously influenced your performance or if you felt you were unprepared. After speaking to fellow test-takers, you might find that everyone found the exam difficult and your percentile range will likely be comparable to your practice exams. Remember, LSAC reports all cancellations.

TRANSCRIPTS

Generally speaking, all law schools require an undergraduate degree for admission. Asked what advice she would give under-grads considering law school, Anne Richard, George Mason's assistant dean and director of admissions, says, "Excel in aca-demics. Although it is important to become involved in activities and be well-rounded, college students should keep in mind that their schoolwork must come first. Use good judgment—don't take on too many activities at the expense of your studies."

Your undergraduate record is a reliable indicator of your ability to succeed in a law program, and it can affect not only your chances of admission but also your financial aid package. Schools nationwide are reporting more and more merit-based scholarship dollars.

Law schools are looking for students with the capacity to think critically and to analyze and synthesize a great deal of information. Traditionally, social science graduates—espe-cially political science, history, and philosophy majors—made up the majority of law school candidates. Today, any rigorous academic preparation that includes logical reasoning, effective communication, and analysis can get you there.

"You're not going to learn to be a lawyer in undergrad, so do things you enjoy. [Even] biology is great preparation for law school. It's rigorous and analytical. Just be sure to com-plement your studies with solid writing and liberal arts courses," says Craig Berry, a graduate of the University of Pennsylvania Law School.

> TIP: If you already have your undergrad sheepskin in hand but your transcript reflects more partying than intellectual pur-suit, all is not lost. Do your best to ace the LSAT. Remember, these scores are even more important without a strong GPA to fall back on.

RECOMMENDATIONS

Your three letters of recommendation are integral parts of your application, so find people who know you and your work abilities well. Most schools prefer that you use the LSDAS recommendation form, and at least one of the three references must come from a professor, preferably one from a rigorous upper-level course.

Give professors and others ample time to complete the recommendations (and don't hesitate to remind professors of the brilliant work you did while in their classes). Ask to review the letters before they are sealed and submitted. A professor may think she is predicting a bright future by expounding on your great unrealized potential, but to an admissions officer that may come across as a sign of laziness. Your recommendations shouldn't make generic comments that don't speak to your academic strengths or to the particular qualities a school may be looking for (your research on schools should give you clues as to what's important).

TIP: Provide your recommenders with your personal statement to ensure a unifying thread throughout your application.

Even if you're applying to law school several years after college, you still have to contact at least one professor. Just e-mail your request, along with your resumé and any recent writing you've done. If you have papers you wrote for that professor, even better.

TIP: Most schools have a credentials service that will keep recommendations on file for students indefinitely after graduation. If you even think you might go to law school, take advantage of it.

PERSONAL STATEMENT

There is no formula for crafting the perfect personal statement. University of Southern California Law School's associate dean of admissions, Bill Hoye, calls the essay a "test of the applicant's advocacy skills—the ability to articulate his or her ideas in a compelling way." Whatever you do, don't follow a preprogrammed approach outlined in a book or on a website. It's not hard to pick out personal statements written by formula. Formulaic approaches fall flat and don't ring true. "Find your own voice," Hoye advises.

Make sure your writing is clear and concise and is a strong statement of your ability to communicate your unique perspective. This is an excellent opportunity to set yourself apart from the masses, so make it count.

> TIP: Be careful not to submit a piece with spelling or grammatical mistakes; after all, you're considering a career where details and technicalities can make or break a case. Have someone proofread your essay.

THE BIG CHOICE

After you've assembled and submitted your killer apps, there's nothing to do but sit back and wait for the results. If you're wait-listed, the best thing to do is just that: wait. Calling the school or attempting to submit other materials won't usually help unless such information is solicited. Once you have your acceptance letters in hand, however, you have some work to do: It's time to decide which school to attend.

Experts agree that visiting a law school is the best way to determine whether you would thrive there. Although you may be tempted to blindly attend the highest ranking school, being on campus will help you make the right decision. "Get a sense of the mood among the student population," says Richard. "It may help you overcome rankings pressure."

Hoye offers this advice: "Contact the faculty and meet with current law students. The way a law school treats you as an applicant suggests the way you will be treated as a student." If you feel welcomed and comfortable, chances are that three years in the company of these people wouldn't be so bad.

And while he lauds the efforts of law schools to improve their marketing efforts, Hoye concedes that it's "hard to convey the personality of a school through a brochure." Go to a class, hang out at a social event, check out the school's resources, and, most of all, talk to people. After the visit, you'll know where you'll be spending the next three years.

RESOURCES

To register for the LSAT, or for more information about the test, go to www.lsac.org.

Before You Go

- Prelaw Prep
- Summer Reading

PRELAW PREP

Because most potential employers look primarily at your first-year grades, the first year of law school is universally considered the most important time for a law student. Put simply, your class rank determines the breadth of career opportunities available to you.

What does this mean? A ferociously competitive pool of people are all aiming for the same goal—to be in the top 10 percent of the class. And they are all looking for any possible means of increasing their chances to be in that select group.

Can law school prep courses help?

Facing her first year of law school, Elizabeth, who was recently accepted at the University of Houston Law Center, was frightened. She would be attending one of the nation's top 50 law schools. The stories she heard about the infamous first year made her wonder whether her native smarts would be enough to propel her to the front of the highly competitive pack.

So on a tip from a friend, Elizabeth signed up for Law Preview, one of a growing number of law school prep courses.

"When you're about to go to law school, everyone has advice, war stories, or tales of what happened to a friend of a friend," says Elizabeth. "It's intimidating and confusing. You don't know what to believe or what strategy to take. I decided that if nothing else, a preview course would give me a plan, and it did."

What's It All About?

Law school preview classes run the gamut from highly organized weeklong sessions to less rigorous one-day workshops. The two main companies battling it out in the marketplace for the law student dollar are BAR/BRI and Law Preview. There are also smaller groups, like those organized by Pace University and the University of Texas.

Law Preview, headquartered in Mount Kisco, New York, was started by four lawyer friends in 1998. The company offers a weeklong course in eight major cities. Students are taught one-day summaries of core law school classes: Contracts, Torts, Property, Civil Procedure, Criminal Law, and Constitutional Law, with optional sessions on legal writing and studying strategies. Before arriving, students are sent a 300-page course book; they're expected to do readings before they begin, and they have homework every night. BAR/BRI, the longer-established of the two and the leader in bar exam preparation courses, has a similar curriculum but also teaches students how to read and brief cases. It offers the course in 11 cities, with a shorter two-day course offered at an additional four locations.

Both courses include some impressive names among their teachers. The workshops have managed to attract an array of well-known professors. Law Preview features a host of top-notch scholars, including Yale torts professor Jules Coleman; Saul Levmore, the dean of the University of Chicago Law School; and Nadine Strossen, president of the American Civil Liberties Union. BAR/BRI boasts John Dwyer, dean at UC-Berkeley's Boalt Hall School of Law, and USC professor

Charles H. Whitebread, renowned for his book *The Eight Se-crets of Top Exam Performance in Law School.*

If you've spent serious money prepping for the LSAT, plunked down more dough for the application fees, and taken out giant loans to help you get through law school, you may find the fees of law school prep courses hard to swallow. For the six-day experience, Law Preview charges $1,075. For those who want basic knowledge but aren't interested in a full week-long immersion, Law Preview offers a one-day legal research and writing workshop for $175. BAR/BRI charges slightly more for its six-day program ($1,175) and its one-day work-shop ($345); its two-day course costs $495.

For Elizabeth, the cost was easily justified. "After you spend more than $1,000 on LSAT prep and you sign your life away to a bank [with student loans], then why not spend an-other $1,100? It couldn't possibly aggravate debt beyond rea-son, and if you do so well in law school that you find yourself in line for one of the 'big' jobs, it would end up paying for it-self," she says.

Other law students, however, are skeptical. "I don't think that it would have been of any assistance to me," says one Yale first-year. "Learning the law is like learning a foreign lan-guage—complete immersion is the only way to get it."

Alternative Means of Preparation

Looking for an alternative to a prep course? First, acquaint yourself with the potential horrors of law school. This means reading Scott Turow's *One L* or watching *The Paper Chase*. Then purchase the Gilberts and the Nutshells—the most pop-ular study aids—for your first-year classes (you can get them online or at a law school bookstore). Read them and get used to the legal terminology. Next, purchase a used textbook, then read a few cases and outline them. Most students agree that it's important to glance at a casebook, just so you know what you're getting yourself into.

SUMMER READING: 40 GREAT
BOOKS TO READ BEFORE YOU GO

Want to bone up further before you're off to school? Read
some of these legal classics.

Classic Literature

The Merchant of Venice
WILLIAM SHAKESPEARE, C. 1594
   One of the master's most performed plays is at its core a
contract dispute over a loan—with the merchant's life hanging in the balance.

Bleak House
CHARLES DICKENS, 1852–1853
   Dickens goes after the English legal system—pretty much
all of it—in what some call his finest work.

Billy Budd, Sailor
HERMAN MELVILLE, 1924 [POSTHUMOUS]
   Melville takes to the sea—the story is set in the British navy
of 1797—where a sailor faces a court-martial and may be put
to death.

The Crucible
ARTHUR MILLER, 1953
   It's the Salem witch trials Miller writes about, but his real
subject is another witch-hunt: McCarthyism.

Inherit the Wind
JEROME LAWRENCE AND ROBERT E. LEE, 1955
   This dramatization of the Scopes monkey trial centers on
the still-controversial legal question of whether Darwinism or
creationism should be taught in schools.

The Apology
PLATO, C. 400 B.C.

Think of it as the ultimate defense argument. Accused of corrupting the young men of Athens, Socrates makes it clear (as Plato retells it) that if seeking the truth corrupts the young, he's guilty.

Crime and Punishment
FYODOR DOSTOEVSKY, 1866

Impoverished Raskolnikov murders an old woman pawnbroker for her money, kills her sister who walks in after the crime, then slowly but surely comes to see that nothing justifies murder.

Pudd'nhead Wilson
MARK TWAIN, 1894

A lawyer rocks a small town in antebellum Missouri during a mistaken-identity murder trial. Twain explores nature versus nurture and points out the real crime: how racial prejudice corrupts justice.

To Kill a Mockingbird
HARPER LEE, 1960

Atticus Finch, a small-town, Depression-era southern attorney, defends a black man accused of raping a white woman and incurs the town's wrath for doing so.

Oresteia
Agamemnon, The Libation Bearers,
The Eumenides
AESCHYLUS, 458 B.C.

The Sopranos have nothing on the Greeks in this centuries-old take on social environment as a cause of criminal behavior.

A Jury of Her Peers
SUSAN GLASPELL, 1917
  In this simple but striking short story, two women hide evidence in a criminal matter, sensing that another woman won't get a fair trial.

The Trial
FRANZ KAFKA, 1925
  A man is charged with something, but he doesn't know what, so he can't prove his innocence. The themes: the power of criminal accusations and the nature of guilt.

Popular Fiction

The Firm
JOHN GRISHAM, 1991
  A young hotshot attorney is lured to a prestigious law firm in the South, where he discovers that a creeping institutional malfeasance lies just behind the mahogany walls.

Presumed Innocent
SCOTT TUROW, 1987
  When a beautiful Chicago district attorney turns up dead, her (married) coworker and former lover is the prime suspect in this legal thriller.

Anatomy of a Murder
ROBERT TRAVER, 1958
  In this courtroom drama, a lone lawyer fights to save a capital defendant accused of committing a vengeance murder after his wife was raped.

The Bonfire of the Vanities
TOM WOLFE, 1990
  In this satire about the intersection of law and politics in New York City, a hit-and-run accident claims as its victim not only the black man who was hit but also the

wealthy investment banker who thought he could get away with it.

The Rumpole Books
JOHN MORTIMER, 1978
   With deft and witty prose, Mortimer creates a British barrister, Horace Rumpole, who's as memorable and entertaining a character as Sherlock Holmes.

Famous Cases

A Civil Action
JONATHAN HARR, 1995
   In a David-versus-Goliath legal battle, plaintiff's attorney Jan Schlichtmann takes on the W.R. Grace Corporation and Beatrice Foods.

In Cold Blood
TRUMAN CAPOTE, 1965
   A small town Kansas family of four is killed by two drifters in this classic true-crime story.

Gideon's Trumpet
ANTHONY LEWIS, 1964
   The story of an innocent Florida convict who wrote to the Supreme Court and established the right to counsel for the poor in America.

The Run of His Life
JEFFREY TOOBIN, 1996
   The best book on the most notorious legal action of the century—the O.J. Simpson murder trial.

Simple Justice: The History of Brown v. Board of Education
RICHARD KLUGER, 1975
   A comprehensive history of the historic Supreme Court decision that marked the beginning of the end of legal segregation.

The Best Defense
ALAN DERSHOWITZ, 1982
In this memoir/legal-adventure tale, the famed criminal defense attorney takes the reader inside some of his most compelling cases.

Legal Theory

American Constitutional Law
LAURENCE H. TRIBE, 1987
Was the Constitution meant to be flexible and subject to judicial interpretation? Or was it meant to be set in stone, changed only when the legislature votes to change it? This is the bible on the subject.

The Brethren: Inside the Supreme Court
BOB WOODWARD AND SCOTT ARMSTRONG, 1979
Rare behind-the-scenes insight into how the nation's most powerful legal institution really works.

The Common Law
OLIVER WENDELL HOLMES, 1881
Drawn from a series of lectures by the iconic Supreme Court justice, this is the definitive guide to Holmes's legal thinking.

Economic Analysis of Law
RICHARD A. POSNER, 1973
Posner wrote the book—and this is it—on the "Chicago school" of law and economics, a.k.a. applying economic thinking to legal decisions to achieve socially desirable outcomes.

The Death of Contract
GRANT GILMORE, 1974
This small but powerful work focuses specifically on contracts, but it's really a way of responding to the ideas about U.S. jurisprudence put forth in *The Common Law*.

Law and the Modern Mind
JEROME FRANK, 1930

In this seminal twentieth-century work, Frank champions the theory of legal realism—that laws should live, breathe, and change, just as humans do.

May It Please the Court: The Most Significant Oral Arguments Made Before the Supreme Court Since 1955
PETER IRONS AND STEPHANIE GUITTON, EDITORS, 1993

Reading the transcripts of landmark cases collected here makes you feel as if you're sitting in the Supreme Court gallery.

The Spirit of Liberty
LEARNED HAND, 1952

Hand may very well be the biggest, best judicial mind never to be tapped for the Supreme Court. *Spirit* is a collection of his papers and rulings.

Taking Rights Seriously
RONALD DWORKIN, 1977

Dworkin, the leading liberal legal scholar, argues for a system of laws based on individual human rights.

Feminism Unmodified
CATHARINE A. MACKINNON, 1987

These controversial essays by the preeminent feminist scholar explore the roots of women's oppression in society and how women themselves contribute to it.

People

Cardozo
ANDREW L. KAUFMAN, 1998

Among other things, Cardozo rewrote tort law and redefined such principles as negligence and assumption of risk. Kaufman's biography mixes legal and personal analysis.

Learned Hand: The Man and the Judge
GERALD GUNTHER, 1994

Gunther offers deep and up-close insight into the life and work of the great American jurist that only a top con-law scholar and former Hand law clerk could.

The Story of My Life
CLARENCE DARROW, 1932

Darrow is a legal legend, and here he writes about his most storied cases—the Scopes monkey trial, Leopold and Loeb, and others.

Law Stories: Law, Meaning, and Violence
GARY BELLOW AND MARTHA MINOW, 1996

Law Stories is a collection of first-person accounts by attorneys working on public-service cases.

Making Civil Rights Law: Thurgood Marshall
and the Supreme Court, 1936–1961
MARK V. TUSHNET, 1994

The definitive biography of the first African-American Supreme Court justice, *Making Civil Rights Law* reveals how Marshall led the fight for racial equality under the law.

Law School

Becoming Gentlemen: Women,
Law School, and Institutional Change
LANI GUINIER WITH MICHELLE FINE AND JANE BALIN, 1997

Based on a study of nearly 1,000 students at the University of Pennsylvania Law School between 1987 and 1992, Guinier argues that law schools treat women unfairly.

Legal Education and the Reproduction of
Hierarchy: A Polemic Against the System
DUNCAN KENNEDY, 1983

A Harvard law professor and a leader of the critical legal studies movement, Kennedy argues that law schools are essentially corporate-lawyer factories, not places of free legal thinking.

The First Year:
Work, Work, Work

- Academics
- Briefing a Case
- The Socratic Method
- Acing Exams
- Social Life
- Making Law Review
- 1L Summer

YES, EVERYONE YOU MEET FEEDS YOU THE SAME HORROR STORY: YOUR FIRST YEAR IN LAW SCHOOL IS GOING TO BE THE TOUGHEST OF YOUR LIFE, COMPLETE WITH MOUNTAINS OF READING, SADISTIC professors, and cutthroat classmates. True enough, generally speaking, but most 1Ls say that the agony is only half the story; hard work and a steep learning curve do come with the territory, but not only is it possible to survive your first year—it's actually possible to enjoy it.

ACADEMICS

First-year students attend class roughly 14 to 15 hours per week. Whether your courses are yearlong or semester-long depends on the school, but the first-year curriculum is virtually identical at every school:

- **Civil Procedure** covers the nuts and bolts of litigation.
- **Torts** covers civil injuries and their remedies, often with a healthy dose of economic theory.
- **Contracts** covers enforceable agreements.
- **Criminal Law** covers criminal statutes and penalties.
- **Constitutional Law** covers the substance and interpretation of the Constitution.
- **Property** covers its ownership and rights.

Most schools also require a first-year seminar in **legal writing and research,** often culminating in a **moot court exercise** where 1Ls argue an imaginary case before a panel of "judges" played by professors or practicing attorneys.

TIP: Law schools generally split the first-year class into sections, and you take all of your classes with your sectionmates. Get to know them well. Though sections disband after the first year, the bonds formed during this period are usually some of the strongest in a law school career.

Here, conventional wisdom has it right: Be prepared to spend loads of time reading. "Nothing prepares you for this much work," says Bethany, a student at Drake University Law School. "I was constantly surprised by how much homework there was." Expect an adjustment period as you learn to read case law, a unique skill that only practice can perfect. "In the beginning of my first year, it took an hour to read and brief a 10-page case," says Deborah, a student at another midwestern law school. "But eventually it becomes second nature." In time, you'll find yourself breezing through cases at warp speed.

BRIEFING A CASE

You're going to be briefing a lot of cases in law school. Briefing is the process of boiling down mountains of facts and legal language into quick summaries. The process of reading, rereading, and analyzing legal texts helps train you to think like a lawyer, says Jeanne Merino, head instructor for first-year legal research and writing at Stanford Law School.

Creating short outlines for each case also helps immensely when you're called on in class; plus, they're an invaluable study aid at exam time.

Some guidelines for briefing cases:

Use shortcuts.   Casebooks have questions after each case, says Jason Criss, an associate at Covington & Burling in New York. Read them first, and keep them in mind. As for "canned briefs"—prewritten notes sold by Gilbert, West, and others—leaning on them to avoid figuring out what's actually important in a case is going to hurt you in the long run, but occasionally using them as study aids doesn't hurt, Criss says.

Read the case. Then read it again.   You won't be able to pick up the key points of the case on the first reading, says Merino. Get an overview, then go back through for details. Then go back through again.

Put the case in context.   Every case is in the book for a reason. The editors choose each case to illustrate an element of law. Understanding why a case was chosen will help you anticipate your professor's questions. "Take a look at the table of contents and figure out, 'Why is this case here?'" Merino says.

Use a set format.   Most 1Ls start out by writing longer narrative case briefs and then later in the year use a shorter, bullet-point style. Whatever style you pick, keep it consistent.

Know the elements.   Most case briefs have seven main parts. The **case name** is self-explanatory; include the name of the court rendering the opinion and the year, says Dana Blatt, author of West Group's *High Court Case Summaries*.

After the case name, list the **facts** of the case. Focus on the facts the court used to support the reasoning of its decision, not the most entertaining facts of the narrative.

The **issue** seems simple, but it has a trick. Select the "single most important [legal] question" in the opinion, framed as a rule of law that isn't confined to the mere facts of the individual case, says Blatt.

The **holding**, or decision, is more simple: How did the court rule?

The court's **rationale** is probably the most important part of a case brief. Summarize the reasons the court ruled as it did, as well as the connection between the facts and the rule, says Blatt.

You'll want to summarize the rationale in **concurrences and dissents** after the majority opinion, too.

Finally, wrap up your brief with some **analysis**. You're not being shown this case solely to learn a rule of law—you're meant to read the judges' words critically, understand where the case fits into legal history, and think about its ramifications and implications. Until you know the kinds of questions your professors typically ask, feel free to ramble a bit here.

Color your life.   Highlighting the different elements of each case in the casebook in different colors can help you if your professor asks a question that isn't in your brief. Don't rely entirely on highlighting, but "there's no great shame, if the professor asks you if a contract was signed in 1930 or 1932, in looking at the page of the casebook," Criss says.

TIP: Before you shell out money for study aids, ask a 2L or 3L for advice and check to see if they're available in the library.

THE SOCRATIC METHOD

If you're the dark-haired woman in the blue sweater three rows from the back, and you've been rudely awakened from your daydream by a law professor's pointing finger, you're probably about to experience the Socratic method. Rest assured that you certainly won't be the first; in fact, the tradition of teaching by question-and-answer session was pioneered by Socrates, who famously engaged his students in dialogue until they reached conclusions incompatible with their original precepts. This type of dialogue forces students to arrive at the answer by gradually building a logical chain, link by link. The goal is to enable you to apply legal reasoning in novel situations instead of merely memorizing the principles behind a given case. Although the strategy is no longer ubiquitous in law schools, it is still a cornerstone of many schools' teaching philosophies, especially in first-year courses.

Students familiar with *The Paper Chase* are likely to associate the Socratic method with Professor Kingsfield's relentless grilling of students in his contracts class, and many may enter law school expecting an experience of both terror and public humiliation. But such scenes are the exception rather than the rule. Real-world Professor Kingsfields still exist, but modern law professors have done much to deemphasize the nastiness of the Socratic technique, and teachers and students alike have increasingly come to understand it as contributing to a collaborative, interactive learning environment in which classes can work together to explore complex legal concepts.

Proponents of the Socratic method argue that the technique is an invaluable training tool because it teaches you how to think like a lawyer. As any practicing attorney knows, real-world legal problems are frequently a great deal more messy and ambiguous than problems that appear in legal textbooks or lectures, and solutions usually only emerge after a protracted and intricate process of analysis, negotiation, argument, and persuasion. Students who learn by Socratic method are considered more likely to emerge from law school confident, articulate, and persuasive in oral argument.

How do you best prepare for the grilling? Some professors call on students in strict alphabetical order; that way, you'll know approximately when your turn is coming, and you'll have an opportunity to prepare lines of argument in advance. However, most professors are not so accommodating: They call on students randomly. In that case, you can't rely on mastery of a particular day's class material to see you through; nor should you rely on cowering at the back of the classroom, hoping the professor won't notice you (he will). The most important things to remember are to stay calm and collected when called upon, to listen attentively to the professor's questions, and to answer as succinctly and persuasively as you can. If you start to panic, you're more likely to lose your thread of argument and babble. Remember that the professor is less interested in testing your knowledge or watching you flail than in provoking an interesting debate from which the entire class can learn. Even if you don't have all the answers to the professor's questions, you can still earn respect by keeping your cool and giving articulate, intelligent responses. The reverse is also true: If you happen to know a great deal about the subject matter, don't cite endless cases to back up your points. Your professor and peers may feel that you're showing off.

What if you're afraid of public speaking? There is no more important phobia to shed, and the sooner you confront it, the better. A career as a lawyer will necessitate a great deal of public speaking—whether in courtrooms or before clients or other lawyers—and a classroom is as good a place as any to practice. The first time may be nerve-racking, but you'll soon hone your skills.

Remember: At most schools, class participation won't affect your grades. "Be prepared for daily classes," says Pedro, a 1L at the University of Illinois, "but focus more on ensuring that you know how to take the exams at the end of the semester."

ACING EXAMS: GRADE-A ADVICE

Speaking of exams . . . the exam period generally lasts for two weeks at the end of each semester. Some schools give students a week of reading days to prepare; others might allot only a weekend for this purpose. Exams are often three hours long, writing-intensive, and sometimes may be taken on your laptop; at some schools, there are take-home exams for which you will be given a set period of time. Here, some advice on how to prepare.

Work Early, Work Often

The number-one mistake students make is to fall behind from the start of the semester, says Robert Miller, the author of *Law School Confidential: A Complete Guide to the Law School Experience.* You got away with it as an undergrad? You will not get away with it here, says Miller. From day one, he advises, block out seven to eight hours every day—try two hours in the morning before classes and five or six hours after dinner—and study during those hours like it's a full-time job. Actually, says Miller, "study like it's more than a full-time job."

Learn to Issue-Spot

Many students try to provide a single answer to an exam question. "They want to sort through the various issues and focus on the determining factor, but they ignore all the other issues," says Henry Noyes, a Pillsbury Winthrop senior attorney and a coauthor of *Acing Your First Year in Law School: The Ten Steps to Success You Won't Learn in Class.* Instead, says Noyes, identify all the key issues, then demonstrate a laserlike analysis of them. Consider the example of a multi-injury car crash: Driver 1 blows a tire and skids across the highway. Talking on his cell phone, Driver 2 slams on his brakes to avoid Driver 1, causing Driver 3 to swerve into another lane and hit Driver 4, a trucker hauling a load of tomatoes. Boom—the road is a wreck-strewn, tomato-slicked MASH unit. The professor asks you to discuss the legal issues with regard to fault. "A bad answer would be to say that you would represent, say, Driver 1, then spend all your time talking about why that person has the best case," says Noyes. A better answer: Spend part of your time assessing each person's case—"what their claims might be and why those claims won't be any good." Was the company that manufactured Driver 1's tires at fault? Was Driver 2 distracted by the cell phone? Was Driver 3 driving too fast or tailgating? Were the tomatoes loaded properly? The more liability issues you spot and analyze, says Noyes, the more points you score. "The professor doesn't care where you end up—she wants to see how you get there."

Outline, Outline, Outline

Want to drive yourself crazy and botch your exams? Try to outline thousands of pages per class the week before finals. Sure, making daily or weekly outlines of your reading takes time and discipline, but, says Miller, regular outlining saves you stress come exam week; it forces you to decide what's essential in a given class; and it helps burn the information into your brain—which means less last-minute memorization, a lousy way to learn. Limit outlines to no more than 70 pages per course, says Miller. "Outlines 300 pages long defeat the purpose." About two weeks before finals, pare down each outline to about eight pages (use diagrams, Miller says, for subjects heavy on prior case law, such as constitutional law, and use bullet-point lists for torts and other courses based on legal principles that can be stated simply in a series of steps). The second outline has all the benefits of the first, and knowing that everything you need to shape an answer is right there on a few pages "keeps you from freezing up."

Go Solo

Study groups sound great in theory: more brainpower, less work, free therapy. But the consensus among experts is to stay away. "Study groups are mostly for people who procrastinate," says Noyes. Too often the get-togethers devolve into gossip and BS sessions where members (whose abilities and work habits tend to vary wildly) show up late, unprepared, nursing a hangover. . . . Instead, find one classmate whom you trust and review complicated cases or your own weak spots with her, advises Miller (bonus: Miller wound up marrying his first-year study partner). And competitive instincts notwithstanding, be willing to lend a hand to others. "What goes around comes around," says Miller.

Study Your Prof

The blind grading system used today at most law schools has put an end to the time-honored tradition of schmoozing your way to the top. Still, it pays to know your instructors' interests. In law school, "you aren't just taking 'Contracts,'" says Charles Whitebread, a University of Southern California professor and the author of *The Eight Secrets of Top Exam Performance in Law School*. "You are taking 'Contracts from Professor X.'" Thus it's important to find out what blows your professor's mental skirt up—and go with it. Has your torts professor published articles about the economic theories of risk allocation? Has he studied the intersection of social psychology and the law? Such pet projects can provide clues about the kinds of exam questions the professor might ask—and the kinds of answers that might impress him. "If a professor must read over and over again a discussion of an issue, it's a good bet that he will ask about an issue that he finds intrinsically interesting," says Whitebread. Look for clues to your instructor's proclivities in old exams, law review articles, and published lectures and speeches. If you can do it subtly, you might point out on the exam ways in which a case you're reviewing relates to your prof's interests.

Chill Out

You're not still studying just before your test, are you? You're not feverishly comparing notes with classmates about what they know and what you don't know, right? You realize it's best to sit quietly and relax before the big moment, yes? Good. We thought so.

Whoa, Speedy

When a test lands on your desk, says Whitebread, take a few minutes to wrap your mind around the basics—the number of questions, how each one is weighted, the amount of time you have to devote to each answer. Next, take 15 minutes or so to think about each question and to sketch your basic thoughts on important points and significant cases. Then—and only then—start writing. Too many students, says Whitebread, dive headlong into the first question, only to realize two-thirds of the way through the exam that they still have four questions to go. Taking 15 to 20 minutes to draw a bead on the whole beast not only averts such disasters but also builds confidence and frees you up to write more compellingly. If you do start to run out of time, write your answers in outline form. The prof will at least get a sense of where you were going.

Kill the Postmortems

A real-life lesson on the wisdom of postexam second-guessing: Scott Parker, a Berkeley, California, sports agent and a Boalt Hall grad, recalls losing sleep over a conversation he'd had with a classmate after his first-year torts final. "The guy said he spotted 47 torts," recalls Parker. "I only spotted four." Panicked, Parker spent the two months before the grades were posted convinced that he had blown the class. Of course, he earned a top grade.

> TIP: Review for common first-year exams by attending bar prep classes. Although you won't take your bar exam until after your third year, many bar review courses are offered for first- and second-year classes to help students synthesize the material.

Grades generally don't come in for at least three to six weeks after the exam. Professors may post grades keyed to anonymous code numbers on a bulletin board in the school, or you may have to call an automated telephone information system to receive them. At some schools, you still get them the old-fashioned way—by mail.

Expect the unexpected when your report card arrives. Most law school courses base grades solely on one do-or-die half-day exam at the end of the semester, and many conscientious students get nasty surprises when they see their grades. Finding yourself in the middle of the curve may be a bitter pill to swallow after the academic success that got you into law school in the first place. But grades "don't mean what they meant in college," says Bethany, a student at Columbia. "Celebrate with a B+, and be ecstatic if you get an A."

The curve varies from school to school. At some, the same percentage of students gets a certain grade on all first-year exams. Some have set policies, so 25 percent of students may get Cs and many more get As. At others, you may find that no one gets a C, but only 3 percent get As.

LIFE—SOCIAL AND OTHERWISE

Yes, you *can* have a life while keeping up with your classes, but by all accounts it's a balancing act. Working too little spells academic disaster. Working nonstop with no outlet for your stress is a recipe for personal misery. "Although it is important to do your best in law school, definitely go out and have a good time," advises Pedro, who plays on a "beer league" basketball team and maintains a busy social life. Intramural sports teams, cultural clubs, and volunteer organizations offer the chance to relax and spend quality time with your classmates. Zachary, a student at Boston University, says his classmates provide a welcome break from the daily grind: "For the most part, everyone is friendly and happy to spend time together inside and outside the classroom."

MAKING LAW REVIEW

As the year comes to a close, you'll probably start hearing people talk about law review.

Supreme Court Justice Sandra Day O'Connor did it. So did Senator Hillary Rodham Clinton. And consumer advocate Ralph Nader. And though it's no guarantee of fame and fortune, it certainly doesn't hurt. "Everyone should do law review," says Brian McDonald, former managing editor of UC-Berkeley's prestigious *California Law Review.* "There is no one type of person that fits the law review mold."

Working on law review is a great way to hone your writing, editing, and analytical skills, as well as an excellent addition to your resumé. Many employers see law review as a sign that you have what it takes to make it in their firm. And while it retains an aura of exclusivity, there are now enough journals on enough subjects that just about any student who wants to do law review can—as long as he or she is smart, hardworking, detail-oriented, and a skilled writer.

What Is Law Review?

Put simply, a law review is a student-run monthly or quarterly academic journal that publishes articles by law professors, law students, judges, and attorneys. At many schools, there are two tiers of journals: those that are more prestigious and competitive (often bearing the name of the school), and several others that are subject-specific (on business law, family law, ethics, intellectual property, and even forensics). Here, answers to frequently asked questions about law review:

How Did Law Review Begin?

Law review was born in 1887, when a group of Harvard students created a journal that would combine student notes on important cases of the day with articles by Harvard faculty and other prominent members of the bar. The journal was called *Harvard Law Review*, and it succeeded so well that there are now hundreds of law reviews published by schools across the United States.

What Kinds of Articles Are Published?

Law reviews tend to follow the format laid out by the *Harvard Law Review* more than a hundred years ago. The *Duke Law Journal*, for example, devotes about a third of each issue to student notes dealing with current legal affairs; the rest is filled with articles by law professors and practicing lawyers.

Law reviews are the main scene of scholarly publishing in legal studies, and as such they are also a major component of legal education. "The best thing about the work is the exposure to cutting-edge issues," says Berkeley's McDonald. "As a top–10 law review, *CLR* receives submissions from the nation's best authors. We evaluate and publish some of the most interesting scholarship available."

Why Do Law Review?

Two words say it all: experience and prestige. As Brian Turetsky, former editor of the *Georgetown Journal of Legal Ethics*, observes, "Any student who wants to research, write, and improve editing and bluebooking skills should consider writing onto a journal. It also happens to be one of the few activities that will remain on your resumé throughout your life. And it's a great way to meet and work with a bunch of people you may not have met yet, especially if you're at a large law school."

In addition to writing case notes and book reviews, students vet submissions, check facts and citations, work with authors to revise and shape accepted pieces, and edit articles to bring them into conformity with *Bluebook* citation standards.

Jeanine Harvey, former publication comanager of the *Michigan Journal of Gender and Law*, explains that law review often "serves as a screening tool for employers, particularly judges, who frankly have more important things to do with their time than sort through transcripts and law school grading policies to figure out where law students stand with respect to their peers."

Indeed, law review has become so synonymous with academic excellence that *not* doing it can send a message to employers that you are not a top candidate—even if you are. As Harvey explains, "Some employers mistakenly view law review as the talisman of a successful lawyer, as if editing a law review perfects one's skills as a litigator, negotiator, or rainmaking partner."

How Do You Make Law Review?

Most law reviews are edited by 2Ls and 3Ls who earn their way onto the journal's editorial staff at the end of their first year of law school. At some schools, invitations to work on law review are issued entirely on the basis of grades (generally the top 10 percent of the first-year class). At others, you can obtain membership by performing well in a writing competition known as a "write-on," regardless of your grades. Still others opt for a combination of these criteria: At the University of Michigan, for example, half of those who make the *Michigan Law Review* do so solely on the basis of their write-ons, and others make it based on the write-on and their first-year grades.

The *California Law Review* has a write-on competition but also looks for qualifications that coursework and writing contests can't measure. "Many people think only the students with the highest grades should be on law review, but that is not how *CLR* views its recruiting process," says McDonald. "Our theory is that a student's performance in class has little or no relation to his or her ability to perform well on law review. It is simply a different world from academia. As such, there is room for all types of law students."

Your reputation among fellow students can thus play a subtle but definite role in your chances of making law review: When evaluating prospective law review members, McDonald says he looks for a number of things that can't be gauged by grades or a writing sample, such as a sharp intellect, tenacity, and a strong work ethic.

How Do Write-Ons Work?

Writing competitions typically take place late in the spring, after the completion of first-year final exams. Though they vary in form from year to year and from one school to another, they usually involve a writing section and an editing section and are graded by review senior editors.

The writing sample showcases your ability to process a large amount of information, formulate a coherent opinion about it, and articulate that view clearly. The editing section demonstrates your ability to transform rocky, ungrammatical writing into smooth, correct prose and how well you can follow the intricate citation guidelines in the *Bluebook*. The personal statement is an exercise in self-presentation, professionalism, and forceful expression. All of it is a test of your ability to work under pressure and to meet deadlines.

Some schools host a single write-on for all reviews, while at others each review handles its own application process. Likewise, selection criteria may vary from year to year. Christian Turner, former president of *Stanford Law Review*, describes a typical set of adjustments: "Last year candidates were selected based solely on a mock edit. We were given an article and told to bluebook a subset of the footnotes and text and to cite-check a smaller subset of footnotes against sources we were provided. This year we brought back, in addition to the mock edit, an essay component, for which candidates wrote a critical response to the piece they edited. The edit involved an 80-page article, of which they edited maybe a third of the footnotes, cite-checking far fewer."

Whatever the format, be creative in your response. "Don't write what they expect to hear," says McDonald. "Your paper will probably be one of 20 that a grader is reading. Make it stand out. Don't be afraid to write something unconventional. They will probably find it refreshing." Whether you are asked to argue a side or to present a balanced analysis of an issue, don't hold back.

Be sure to set aside a block of time between exams and the start of your summer job to complete the task. "Take a break after you finish finals, and then discipline yourself to sit down and do it," Turetsky advises. It's no fun trying to squeeze your write-on entry into a hectic schedule, especially when you consider that you only have one shot at selling yourself. At most journals, if you don't make it after year one, you won't have a chance to try again.

"It's kind of like pledging a fraternity," Turetsky recalls. "If you want to be a member, you have to go through a not-so-pleasant experience. After the thrill of finishing your first year of law school, picking up the write-on packet is like getting kicked in the stomach. I had a family wedding in the middle of the write-on period, so I was in a hotel with all these cousins I hadn't seen in years, and I couldn't hang out with them because I had to write a paper on kiddie porn. Not my idea of a good time."

How Do You Balance Law Review and Coursework?

Law review can be rewarding, but it's also time-consuming. "Even the most prepared find themselves scrambling to get their law review work done in addition to their normal class-work," says McDonald.

Publication deadlines, after all, don't yield to academic schedules, and few authors submit work that is in good shape *Bluebook*-wise. While senior editors work with the author to clean up any problems with an article's content, it's up to the 2L member editors to make sure that an article's footnotes are accurate and correctly cited. By the time proofs go to the author, an article will have been checked and edited at least twice.

So how are jobs distributed? Turner describes a typical breakdown: "Our second-year members are assigned to editing teams that divide tasks associated with accepted articles. Third-year members can opt to join staffs (selection of articles, student notes, or book reviews; symposium planning) or run for a position as an officer on the managing board," he explains. "For the [2L] member editor, we try to assign a reasonable number of edits over the course of a year. The work comes in spurts, although we try to smooth things out, avoiding high-pressure times during the year. The daily grind is up to the student—a little bit of cite-checking and library work each day for a week or two, or a marathon couple of days. My gut tells me that most law students fall into the latter camp."

The Bottom Line

If law review sounds like an experience you want to avoid, don't worry. "Many students seem to feel obligated to join a journal even if they really don't want to be on one," says Turetsky. If that's the case, he says, "find some other avenue to get some writing experience that you'd enjoy more. But you should also take a look at where you want to work; there may be judges and firms and other future employers that use journal membership as a litmus test. Make sure you have all the information you need—and understand the consequences if you choose to pass on the experience."

WHAT TO DO DURING 1L SUMMER

The summer after the first year of law school used to be a time for students to do something quirky—or do nothing at all. According to Jacquelyn Burt, assistant dean for placement at Cardozo Law School's Center for Professional Development, "students don't have that luxury anymore." Forget canning salmon in Alaska; if you can get into a law firm, do it. "And work hard once you're there," says Burt.

Working at a firm after your first year signals eagerness. "It gives you some perspective," says Susan Gainen, director of career services at the University of Minnesota Law School. "You'll get to see how law is practiced." Better yet, you'll actually get some experience in practicing law, "particularly if you find a firm that gives 1Ls substantive assignments," says Audrey Rohan, a hiring partner at New York's O'Sullivan LLP.

A 1L summer spent indoors is an especially wise strategy if your grades aren't great—a foot in the door and extra effort can pump up a resumé with a flabby GPA. And depending on your performance at a firm, you just might clinch an offer for the next summer well before any of your classmates do. "I've had students who received offers for the second summer, and some for permanent jobs after law school," says Gainen. Even if you intend to shop around a bit for that 2L or permanent job, an offer extended from another firm and references from its lawyers can only help.

Because law firms don't typically interview 1Ls on campus, you'll have to take the initiative. Your school's career office might have information about firms that are doing more hiring among 1Ls (a growing number are). The NALP directory of legal employers is one of the best resources here—it lists the major firms throughout the country, indicating whether or not they hire 1Ls. Otherwise, use your networking contacts (good practice for later) and law firm guides available at bookstores and online to identify, say, 15 firms that appeal to you. Check the firms' websites for information about recruiting and hiring contacts, then send off resumés, with cover letters explaining your interest. Keep it simple, suggests Joanne DeZego, director of recruitment at New York's Milbank, Tweed, Hadley & McCloy. "And don't do anything cute that you think might get attention."

If you know the firm hires 1Ls, simply express your interest in applying for a position, say why you're interested in the firm, and spell out your qualifications. If the firm doesn't typically hire 1Ls, say something such as, "I'm aware that your firm doesn't typically hire first-year law students, but I'm extremely interested in working at the firm and would welcome an opportunity to talk about what, if anything, I could do there this summer." You might be surprised at the response.

Many lawyers will be impressed by your initiative and your interest in committing to their firm so early. Even if you don't get hired, you'll be able to refer to your early eagerness if you interview with them as a 2L.

Also, suggests Gainen, consider going home for that first summer. "If 'home' is a place where big firms will hire 1Ls from out of town, that's a great thing to do," she says. You might be considering moving back to your hometown, and for that one summer it can even be a way to make, and save, some extra money—sublet your law school apartment, move back in with the folks, and put those weekly checks in the bank. Firms that do hire 1Ls generally pay them at the same rate as 2Ls.

If you can't land a paying job, and if you can swing it financially, consider an internship. Slave labor? You bet. But the experience could put you ahead of the pack when it's time to interview for 2L jobs.

7

The Second Year:
Land a Job

....

- Academics
- Extracurriculars
- The Recruiting Process
- Interviewing 101
- Answering Interview Questions
- Recruiting Meals
- Etiquette
- Clerkships
- Summer Associate Wisdom
- Summer Associate Don'ts

IN SEPTEMBER OF YOUR SECOND YEAR, THE ONSLAUGHT OF EX-
TRACURRICULARS AND JOB-HUNTING PICK UP WHERE ACADEMICS
LEFT OFF IN MAY. YOUR SECOND YEAR IS UNLIKELY TO BE AS
nerve-racking as your first, but in many ways, it's just as
tough.

ACADEMICS

There's a knack to taking law school courses, and by the time
your second year rolls around, you'll finally feel like you
know what you're doing. "Expect that the material will probably come a little more easily," says Sam, a student at Boston

University School of Law. More good news about your second-year classes: You pick them yourself. After a year of being force-fed civil procedure, torts, and contracts, the opportunity to take courses of your own choosing is a welcome change.

Douglas, a student at Boston College Law School, finds his second-year classes "definitely more interesting and rewarding," in part because they allow students to "explore their own interests and focus on specific issues that a general first-year course cannot consider."

TIP: If your law school allows you to cross-register for courses in other parts of the university, take advantage of it. A course in business, government, or a foreign language adds perspective to your legal education and gives you the opportunity to meet graduate students in other disciplines.

EXTRACURRICULARS
Moot Court

Moot court is an extracurricular option that can impress potential employers; it's a step closer to the real work lawyers do. Most schools field mock trial teams who argue fictitious cases in nationwide tournaments. Many also offer intramural appellate competitions, where groups of students prepare and argue simulated Supreme Court cases. These activities are especially valuable if you intend to go into litigation.

Clinical Programs: Bringing the Law to Life

On-the-job training, long a requirement in professional fields such as medicine, social work, and education, did not become standard practice in law schools until the 1970s. Today, however, almost all law schools offer second- and third-year students the opportunity to participate in clinical placements as part of their legal education. Conducted under the supervision of law school faculty and/or practicing attorneys, these programs offer participants the chance to gain hands-on experience with clients, cases, and courts.

Not all law students choose to participate in clinical programs, but if you find your classes frustratingly theoretical, or if you simply want a chance to apply what you're learning to real-world situations, consider signing up. The range of experience may include interviewing and counseling clients; drafting pleadings and briefs; managing cases; and participating in preliminary hearings, trials, and appeals.

In addition to learning a useful set of skills, you may have the opportunity to help worthwhile organizations. Whether dealing with the poor, victims of domestic violence, prisoners, political refugees, or AIDS patients, law students in clinical placement tend to represent those people who desperately need legal assistance but cannot afford the services of full-time practicing attorneys.

The exact scope and nature of clinics vary according to individual schools' traditions, strengths, and interests. At the University of California–Berkeley's Boalt Hall, for example, law students may participate in the Death Penalty Clinic, which provides legal counsel to prisoners facing capital punishment in the state of California; in the International Human Rights Law Clinic, which assists refugees seeking asylum in the United States and works with organizations worldwide to oppose human rights violations; and in the Samuelson Law, Technology, and Public Policy Clinic, which, taking advantage of Berkeley's traditional strength in technology law, represents the public interest in electronic civil liberties issues such as Internet free speech and online privacy.

Under the aegis of its long-standing Law in Action program, the University of Wisconsin Law School hosts several different clinical initiatives, including the Frank J. Remington Center, the Legal Defense Program, the Public Defender Project, the Consumer Law Litigation Clinic, and the Family Law Project.

Representing the legal needs of battered women, terminally ill patients, or prisoners on death row may be emotionally exhausting, but participants in clinical programs generally derive a sense of personal and professional satisfaction from helping people in need. Indeed, clinical experience often gives young lawyers a commitment to public service.

THE RECRUITING PROCESS

Deep down, the professors know it: Until 2Ls have their summer offers, no one is paying much attention in class. That's one reason law schools keep moving up the fall recruiting season; at some, like New York's Brooklyn Law School, on-campus interviewing begins as early as August.

Recruiting exposes the naked elitism of the legal profession. Top firms may refuse to interview students whose GPAs are below a certain cutoff, and they adjust that cutoff based on the name of the school. For example, a firm might grant interviews to students at second-tier schools only if they have GPAs of 3.7 or above and are members of the law review; to students at top-20 schools only if they have a 3.3 or above; and to any interested student who attends Yale, Stanford, or Harvard.

TIP: Some firms shun certain schools altogether. But never be shy about contacting a firm that doesn't recruit at your school; you have nothing to lose but one copy of your resumé.

Signing up for on-campus interviews is usually easy: All you have to do is submit a resume. If there are many options available, choosing firms can be challenging. The number of firms recruiting at each school varies, but most students interview with 10 to 30. The pressure to choose wisely is high; 2L summer jobs usually turn into offers for full-time work, and many firms hire only those students who have worked for them in the summer.

> TIP: Talk to as many 3Ls as possible about their experiences at various firms, and do as much independent research as you can. Three good resources: your career placement office, law firm websites, and jdjungle.com.

INTERVIEWING 101

Landing a plum position at a law firm generally entails undergoing a rigorous series of interviews. This is your chance to make an impression above and beyond your glowing resumé. Here's how to make the most of the opportunity.

Round One: The Screening Interview

If they hire 1Ls at all, firms generally skip on-campus interviews in the first year, preferring to see your resumé and evaluate you in person when you're in town. But when you're a 2L, the interview process heats up—and often moves to campus.

Depending on your school, there might be a lottery process to sign up for screening interviews, the first round of evaluation that's used primarily to confirm initial expectations about you based on your credentials. Generally, you can rank firms in order of preference when you sign up. In the lottery system, you can't be rejected outright based on your resumé, so even mediocre students might get their 15 minutes with a recruiter from a top-ranked law firm.

> TIP: Even if you don't win a scheduled audience with your firm of choice, persistence (even a simple phone call to the recruiting contact) can gain you a spot.

Prepare Yourself

Before the big day, do your homework. Sunny, a recent law school grad and current federal court clerk who accepted an offer at a prominent Silicon Valley law firm, offers the following advice: "Know the firm, the practice, and, if possible, the attorney you're talking to—bios are often offered in the hospitality rooms [waiting areas, usually stocked with refreshments] or on the firm's Web site."

Learn as much as possible about the kind of work the firm does. Interviewers are impressed when you show them that you know what their firm has to offer. They won't be thrilled if you gush about your interest in a practice area that they don't have.

Check out the National Association for Law Placement form on the particular office of the firm at which you are interviewing. Many firms' branch offices have stats different from the headquarters, especially when it comes to practice areas and attorney demographics. Your career services office should also have useful material, such as employer evaluations from years past.

Classmates and alumni are another invaluable resource— talk to people who have worked at your target firm. They can give you the lowdown on what it's like to work there. Sometimes this is the only way to find out about a firm's less desirable aspects.

Dress the Part

A professional appearance alone won't land you the job, but a sloppy one will certainly hurt your chances. Some employers state that students may attend interviews in business-casual attire. Many interviewers, however, would still prefer to see you in a suit. Because firms often send multiple interviewers of varying ages and degrees of conservatism to on-campus recruiting events, your best bet is to stick with the suit.

Carry a leather portfolio, and bring extra copies of your resumé and transcript. Even if they have everything, interviewers may ask you for an additional copy just to see if you're prepared.

Sell Your Strengths

The screening interviewer generally has only about 20 minutes per candidate and has probably already formed an opinion—based on your resume, transcript, and sometimes a legal-writing sample with case citations—about whether to invite you to the firm for a callback. In general, if the interviewer has already decided that you've got the right stuff and should be called back, you have to do something really over the top to lose the chance. On the flip side, if you're not up to muster on paper, there's usually little you can do to change the interviewer's mind. If you're on the borderline, though, let your dazzling interview skills shine.

Enoch Chang, a former member of the recruiting committee at Bingham McCutchen, says, "Be yourself. When you try to create an image that's not really you or to fit into a preconceived image of what the firm wants, the interviewer will see right through it."

Don't feel pressured to discuss law-related topics. One 3L at Georgetown was surprised when her screening interviewers seemed more taken with her oboe playing than her law journal work or favorite courses. Following their lead, however, she discussed wind instruments as long as they seemed interested. She got a callback—and an offer. The bottom line: If you and your interviewer have a common passion for opera, you'll score far more points—and make a more lasting impression—discussing the finer points of *La Traviata* than Rule 23.

Be Flexible

What if your interviewer begins with a vague question such as: "So, what can I tell you about the firm?" Rather than jumping into a question-and-answer session right away, be prepared with a three- to five-minute narrative that neatly presents both who you are and where your interests in the firm lie. Begin with a statement that addresses the question, and then tie that into your story.

John Kuehn, a hiring partner at Kirkland & Ellis in New York, recommends that you highlight "an issue about which you are writing a paper or journal article, something from moot court, or a legal question you wrestled with during your 1L summer internship. You can use the same story or two over and over again from interview to interview, but if you do, present it a bit differently each time so you don't sound 'scripted.'"

Location, Location, Location

If you grew up in Seattle, you'll have no difficulty proving your intention to return there. But if you spent your entire life in Los Angeles, interviewers may be skeptical about your sudden desire to work in, say, Boston. Mark Weber, director of career services at Harvard Law School and former assistant dean for career services at the University of Illinois College of Law, suggests the following strategy if you don't have any ties to the target city: "Put your money where your mouth is. Visit the city, and, if possible, try to arrange brief meetings with the firms that you're interested in. Even a casual vacation can turn into an interview offer if you seem truly bent on going to that city. Firms are making an investment in you when they train you in the first year. If you can't prove that you're serious about staying, the firm isn't going to gamble all that time and money."

Kuehn warns, however, that "you don't want it to look as if you merely signed up to interview with every firm in the relevant city that comes to your campus." Make sure you have an arsenal of firm-specific comments—that go beyond geography—to use in response to the inevitable question: "Why did you sign up to interview here?"

Put on a Happy Face

Did you hate your civil procedure course? Now isn't the time to say so. It's far smarter to talk about the insightful professor, the interesting subject matter, and your intelligent classmates.

Interviewers don't like any hint of a negative attitude. Demonstrate that you can find silver linings in the stormiest of legal clouds: "Try to describe what was positive about the experience, even if you disliked it. If you didn't get along with your 1L summer employer, don't bash them in future interviews. As far as the firm is concerned, you'll probably be saying the same things about them next year," says Weber.

Round Two: The Callback Interview

Congratulations if you've made it to this stage. Firms will generally let you know via telephone if you've made callbacks, by mail if the answer's no.

The primary purpose of the callback—usually held at the firm—is to confirm the screening interviewer's impression of you and to determine whether your personality is a good match. According to Kuehn, the difference between the screening and callback interviews can be summed up as follows: "On campus, the question is, 'Does this candidate merit a more in-depth examination?' During the callback, it's 'Would I really want to work with this candidate?'"

The usual method of testing your "fit" is to have you interview with four to six attorneys, half of whom will usually be partners, and then send you off to lunch with two junior associates. Sunny warns, "During the callback, you have to sustain your energy, edge, and enthusiasm for a half—or a whole—day. That's the biggest challenge."

Give . . . and Take

While the screening interview is more about selling yourself to the firm, the callback round is a forum in which you can not only hype yourself but also satisfy your curiosities about your potential employer. Since each interview in the callback phase is generally about 30 minutes long, you should have time to both talk about yourself and ask questions about the firm.

Avoid sounding canned in your inquiries. When the interviewer hears "Tell me about your summer program" for the hundredth time, her response is likely to be uninspired. Instead, consider asking questions designed to elicit the information you want in a less obvious manner. Weber suggests the following: "Instead of asking how much responsibility young associates are given (the stock response will be 'A lot'), ask the interviewer about a current project she is working on, and then ask how she assigns or is assigned work, and if it is substantive."

Express your interest in that particular firm. If you want to take part in its pro bono activities during the summer, tell your interviewers. If it has a special litigation training camp you're interested in attending, let them know. Interviewers are always impressed when you demonstrate genuine interest and at least an inkling of what practice areas or unique firm feature you would like to explore as a summer associate.

Do Some Digging

As you go through the day, ask relevant questions about training, mentoring, partner contact, and feedback on assignments. The truly hard-core might inquire about the partnership track: What's the process and timeline for making partner at the firm? Are there different tracks (junior versus senior partners, nonequity versus equity partners)? How many people make partner each year? Also ask (in a diplomatic way) about the attorneys' lifestyle: number of hours worked, billing requirements, workload, level of responsibility, variety of work, compensation, morale. "If the lawyer is a lateral [hire] at the firm," Kuehn adds, "ask him or her to compare the experience at this firm with the other."

Size up the senior associates and partners. After meeting them, ask yourself if they typify the kind of lawyer you'd like to be in a few years. Also ask the younger associates why they chose this firm over others like it. Ideally, they will give you the lowdown on many of the same places you are also interviewing at. Note: If they bash other firms, chances are that their firm isn't a great place to work; lawyers at top firms don't put down their competitors.

Be Tactful

If there's something controversial about the firm that you want to know about, there are two things to keep in mind. First, if it's really important to you, you should probably ask about it—you won't be happy at the firm if you don't. Second, if it's not that important to you but you still want to know, hold off until you have an offer in hand. Still, when asking the question (e.g., "Why is there such a low percentage of minority partners?" or "Will I have to defend tobacco corporations?"), Weber notes that the issue is not "what is asked, but how it is asked. Ask the interviewers for their take on the subject, but don't be hostile or defensive." Focus on learning about the issue, not on airing your grievances.

Never ask about benefits. "'What's in it for me?' questions are premature at this stage and are irrelevant until an offer is on the table. It will look . . . like you're focused on all the wrong things, and you might come across as greedy," warns Weber.

Honesty Is the Best Policy

Never pretend to know something—or someone—that you don't really know. Kuehn illustrates this with an amusing anecdote: "Some time ago, during a callback interview with a 2L interested in bankruptcy work, one of my partners mentioned a publication that our bankruptcy department writes and sends to clients and law schools. The candidate enthusiastically reported that he was familiar with the publication and had been reading it for 'years.' In fact, the bankruptcy group had just recently put out the second quarterly edition ever. No offer, of course."

If you're interviewing in your 3L year because you didn't get an offer from your 2L employer, don't dodge the issue, says Weber. "Relate what happened in a positive light. Explain what you learned over the summer, and if the reason you didn't get an offer was because you didn't 'fit' with the firm, reassure the interviewer that you have the ability to do the work, and consider getting a reference from your former employer who can at least attest to your work product."

Don't Forget Your Manners

Although you may feel more comfortable asking certain questions of the younger associates, treat all the attorneys with the same level of respect. Recruiters often present the lunch hour—usually spent with more junior attorneys—as separate from the rest of the day, but don't let down your guard. You are still being evaluated and should treat the meal just as you would another office interview. While "you don't have to spend the entire lunch period talking about the firm," says Kuehn, "spending no time doing so suggests that you aren't really interested. Your lunchmates will convey this to the more senior attorneys. Don't assume that the lawyers making offer decisions will ignore the impressions of the younger attorneys. These are your prospective peers; if they don't like you, that hurts your chances."

The lunch might also be used as a measure of your fit in an egalitarian culture. "Exercise good table manners and be polite to the waitstaff. Saying 'Please' and 'Thank you' will go a long way in furthering your cause," says Chang. "Moreover, general politeness will reflect on how you will interact with other people in the firm, particularly the support staff."

Case the Joint

As you are being escorted around the firm, observe the atmosphere. Do people seem happy there? Are people outside of their offices and chatting by the coffeemaker? Does the support staff seem content? When you're being taken from office to office for interviews, do the attorneys know where they're going? Are they acquainted with the lawyer you're speaking to next? Ask yourself if you'd be comfortable spending your days—and quite possibly nights—in that space.

Tie Up Loose Ends

After your callback day, write thank-you notes to the firms you interviewed with. At least for your top-choice firms, a handwritten note is a nice gesture that demonstrates your sincere interest. Because you may meet several people at each firm, send a note to the recruiting partner, asking him or her to convey your regards to the others.

Once you have offers in hand, don't vanish! Keep in touch with your contact person at each firm, and be sure to check in now and then to let them know where you stand with your decision. Remember that there are a lot of people who would love to take one of the offers you are holding. If you are certain you are not going to take an offer, decline it immediately.

Final Words

"Remember that recruiting is a two-way process," says Kuehn. "The firm is as much a candidate that you are interviewing as the other way around. The firm only makes the preliminary decisions—whether to extend a callback and make an offer. You decide which offer to take. You need to elicit what information you can from your 'candidates' so you can make that decision. Too many students get to the last step and can't distinguish between firms. Ask questions throughout the process. If need be, after you've received an offer, ask to make a return visit to the office, or to talk to more lawyers on the phone.

"Also, relax. Although a few 2Ls end up accepting offers with firms with whom they spend many years after law school, that's the exception, not the rule. The recruiting process is highly subjective, and the information exchanged is usually selective, for both the firm and the student. The only way for you and a firm to really determine whether you are right for each other is for you to work there for a couple of years. Take the selection process seriously, but don't add pressure by thinking that a wrong step will cause irreparable damage."

TALK SMART: HOW TO ANSWER INTERVIEW QUESTIONS

Of all the skills required in an interview, the most important is to know how to *answer the questions*. This sounds simple. It is not.

We asked a panel of top legal experts to share with us their favorite interview questions. Then we had real law students give their answers.

The pros then graciously evaluated the students' responses and offered expert advice on how to impress the best.

THE PANEL

JeanMarie Campbell
Manager of recruitment and professional development
Akin, Gump, Strauss, Hauer & Feld
Kim Koopersmith
Hiring partner
Akin, Gump, Strauss, Hauer & Feld
Andrew Rossman
Partner and hiring committee member
Akin, Gump, Strauss, Hauer & Feld
Gail Flesher
Partner and recruiting committee chair
Davis Polk & Wardwell

Michele Jawin
Director of partners, groups, mergers
Mestel & Company

What got you interested in the law?

"I've been exposed to the law my whole life. A lot of my family members are lawyers."

—New York University 1L

"The intellectual stimulation and wanting to help people. Also, the reputation."

—Boston University 2L

"My parents said I'd make a good lawyer because I like to argue and debate. But it wasn't until I was a paralegal—I worked on real estate transactions and foreclosures—that I realized I truly liked the profession."

—Rutgers-Camden 1L

Bad

Playing the family card ("A lot of family members are lawyers") or the natural aptitudes card ("I like to argue and debate") may be logical enough from a student's point of view, but recruiters hate both tactics. They're overused, and interviewers are sick of hearing them. Plus, family stories show "intellectual laziness," says Gail Flesher, chair of the recruiting committee at New York's Davis Polk & Wardwell. Talking about your parents marks you as juvenile, and "Also, the reputation" is flat-out off-putting. "Like it appeals to the girls or the boys in the bar? That wouldn't fly with me," says Michele Jawin, an executive with Mestel & Company, a recruiting firm based in New York and Washington, D.C. In general, the answers aren't nearly specific enough about each student's unique motivation. To succeed at a law firm, says Kim Koopersmith, a hiring partner at Akin, Gump, Strauss, Hauer & Feld in New York, "you have to really want to do this. It's not an easy way to make a living, so you had better have thought it through on your own."

Good

The last piece of the Rutgers 1L's answer establishes the kind of personal connection that recruiters are looking for, says member Andrew Rossman, a partner and hiring committee member at Akin, Gump. Saying "I was a paralegal [and] I realized I truly liked the profession" may not seem like a home-run answer, but it doesn't have to be. The point is, the student took a firsthand experience and related it to her decision to become a lawyer. "That's real," says Rossman. "That I can accept."

The Bottom Line

Be prepared to talk about a concrete personal experience that led you to the law. If you have something big, great—go with it. JeanMarie Campbell, Akin, Gump's manager of legal recruitment and professional development, recalls one student, for instance, whose parents were killed in an accident; a lawyer helped the student with estate and finance issues, and that inspired her to go into the law. But you don't have to have the slam-dunk reason. Recruiters realize that most law students have had neither much practical legal experience nor a life-altering episode that drew them to the field. Just be sure your reason paints you in a flattering light. Consider the BU 2L's answer about "intellectual stimulation." "If that's true, that's perfect," says Flesher. "If you worked as a paralegal, great. You have to have a reason, though. There's got to be a reason."

Why do you want to work in a law firm?

"Working in a firm will expose me to many practice areas and different partners and associates."

—NYU 1L

"I'll grow and learn the most in a firm environment. I want to learn different areas of law because I feel I'm too young to commit myself to one specialty."

—BU 2L

"When I worked for a law firm in Florida, I liked the opportunity to help the client. I also liked when the attorneys brought in novel problems and issues. I realize that a corporate environment would offer the same type of problem-solving opportunities, but a law firm will offer more diversity as to the types of problems and the opportunities to help clients."

—Rutgers-Camden 1L

Bad

Me, me, me. You're definitely on the wrong track if your answer implies that a firm should cater to your desires (see "Working in a firm will expose me to many practice areas," and "I'll grow and learn the most in a firm environment"). To an interviewer, this says you're less interested in helping the firm than you are in helping yourself. It may also imply that you're there to get your basic training, then leave. Yes, you need to find out what the firm can do for you, but do it later, after you get an offer. For now, show the interviewer what you can do for the firm. Another problem: "None of these answers says anything about the business," says Flesher. "There's lots about the work that should be interesting to the applicants, and if it's not, they shouldn't be going to a firm." Yet another mistake: the way the Rutgers 1L mentioned "a corporate environment" out of nowhere. The remark sends a signal that she may be as interested in business as she is in law.

Good

The Rutgers 1L tried to connect her answer to a real-world experience that had inspired her to work for a firm.

The panelists agree, however, that she should have gone deeper, citing specific cases or matters that she worked on.

The Bottom Line

As with the first question, be prepared to answer this one by citing a personal experience—in this case, one that made you want to work at a law firm (as opposed to, say, a DA's office). Also key to acing this query: Show that you understand the complexity and challenges of practicing law at a firm. After all, why would anyone believe you when you say you'd be good at a job if you don't know what the job entails? Vague answers about "many practice areas" and "different partners" only serve to show how little you know. Instead, talk about a case that the firm has worked on recently, say why you found that matter interesting, and spell out how you could see yourself enjoying— and contributing to—that sort of work. Try something like: "The *Stumpington* case you handled is obviously going to have a major impact on IP law. That sort of matter is something I think I could contribute to, because. . . ." No one expects you to be an expert, but don't present yourself as utterly naïve either. Instead of "I'm too young to commit myself to one specialty," at least try something like "I think my skills and interests could be a good match for your litigation department," says Rossman.

What drew you specifically to our firm?

"I'm attracted to firms that have a bicoastal presence, because I'm from California. I'm also interested in a firm that does all kinds of work, because I'm unsure about what I want to do right now."

—NYU 1L

"I was attracted to your firm because of its great reputation. And it's in the location I want to settle in."

—BU 2L

"I want the opportunity to work in New York City and to try different areas of the law before settling down and developing an expertise in one or two areas."

—Rutgers-Camden 1L

Bad

A firm with a "bicoastal presence"? One with a "great reputation"? "In New York City"? The students are describing some 50-odd firms, the panelists point out. "One question I ask in our evaluations is 'Interest in the firm?'" says Rossman. "I have no basis to say that the BU 2L has a particular interest in my firm."

Good

Sorry, thanks for playing.

The Bottom Line

There's no excuse for not knowing what a given firm has to offer—or not being prepared to say what about the firm appeals to you. These days, firm websites detail everything from practice groups to starting salaries; stories about firms in legal publications are easily accessible on the Internet; and online forums like Greedy Associates offer all manner of inside scoop. Gathering even a few tidbits from these sources will show an interviewer that you've done some homework. Better yet, use your networking skills to make contact with a lawyer at the firm and ask her questions. Saying "I spoke to one of your associates the other day, and one of the things I learned was . . ." is an excellent way to show that you care enough about a firm to go the extra mile. Next, says Koopersmith, "make a presentation that explains why this firm is what you're looking for. Say, 'I like that you have an international practice' or 'I like that you staff the litigation department in a particular way.' With me, that scores points." Another tip: Avoid expressing your interest in one firm by making negative comments about another. Plain and simple, it's unprofessional.

What did you do last summer?

"I just temped to make some extra money. It was pretty administrative, but I learned a lot about hedge funds, because my boss was meeting with investors, trying to get them to invest."

—NYU 1L

"I worked for the Suffolk County district attorney's office in Boston, doing legal research. I used creative skills and also skills I learned as a law student. I approached every situation as a search-and-rescue mission and saw myself as a man my supervisors could depend on."

—BU 2L

"I was on a study-abroad program in Beijing. Learning about the differences and similarities between our laws and theirs was fascinating. And developing relationships with the students and professors as well as local residents was thrilling."

—Rutgers-Camden 1L

Bad

Oh, where to begin? Let's start with, "I just temped." "That's just dumb," says Flesher. "And lazy." It's not that there's anything wrong with temping, but use the experience to focus on something substantive, she says. The NYU 1L was headed in a better direction, for example, when she mentioned learning about hedge funds. But her answer would have been far stronger if she had gone deeper into the specifics of what she learned and how that knowledge affected her interest in the law. Give a demerit to the BU student for the phrases "search-and-rescue mission" and "a man my supervisors could depend on." Both remarks cross the line between self-confident and cocky, the panelists say. (In general, simply state the facts about anything you've accomplished and let the interviewer draw his or her own conclusions.) The Rutgers 1L, our hero to date, whiffed this question badly. Calling a cross-cultural learning experience "fascinating" comes off as glib and unsophisticated, the panelists say. Interviewers don't care whether you liked your coworkers or bosses. Those answers relate to people skills. And as Flesher says, "We're judging your people skills just by talking to you, so focus on substance."

Good

The BU 2L was smart to bring up his Suffolk County job. You've certainly got a leg up if you spent your summer working in a DA's office or, for that matter, any law-related job (note: do that). The trouble? You guessed it—lack of specifics. Rossman's suggestion: "Say something like 'There was a case that involved kidnapping. There was an interstate jurisdictional issue about whether you could prosecute someone you know who kidnapped a person in Massachusetts and took them to Rhode Island. I researched it and wrote a memo.'" That speaks volumes about a candidate, Rossman says—what she's done, how she explains matters, how involved she got in the work. "Show me that you're thinking."

The Bottom Line

Koopersmith has a tip that applies to the "just temped" answer—and to all answers, in fact. Before you start talking, take a few seconds to organize your response. The "just temped" answer would have been much better, she says, "if the student had paused and started simply with 'I had an opportunity to work in the hedge fund area, and it exposed me to an area of corporate practice I might be interested in.'"

How will law school help you as a lawyer?

"I feel that my law school education will be invaluable regardless of what I do."

—*NYU 1L*

"My student government experience helped me with my people skills, and my clinic experience taught me how to interview and counsel clients. It also taught me that details should not be overlooked."

—*BU 2L*

"My law school education will open doors for me. With a law degree, the possibilities are virtually unlimited as to what avenues I can explore."

—*Rutgers-Camden 1L*

Bad

The NYU student's ship is sinking fast. If by now you don't recognize the gross failings of that answer (vague, impersonal), your boat will likely go down, too. The BU 2L's answer may appear to be good, but at least part of it is flawed, says Koopersmith. If you have to talk about student government, she says, "it shows you don't have enough substance." Once again, the Rutgers student has accidentally revealed that the law may not really be a main interest. Her comment about law school's opening doors translates as a lack of commitment to legal work, says Jawin. "That makes me nervous. I want to hear something definite about wanting to be a lawyer."

Good

The clarity with which the BU student delivered his remarks about his student government and clinic work showed that he had come prepared (that said, be careful that your answers don't sound canned, even if you've given them a dozen times already). And the law clinic work that the BU student refers to is a solid response. To a law firm, almost any hands-on real-world experience you get in law school is a big plus. That said—have we mentioned this before?—the student could have been more substantive and specific.

The Bottom Line

In a way, the "How will law school help you?" query is a trick question. If all you have to talk about is what classes and professors you liked or what you did on student government, you're not going to impress anyone. If you don't have practical experience, translate what you've learned in a class into something that shows why you're interested in—or why you'll be good at—working for a law firm. Try something like "I had a class in which we talked about telecom deals that involved big firms. The most interesting case was X. What I learned was Y. That's exactly the kind of work I think I'd like to do." Or talk about a professor in terms of how she got you interested in an area of the law. "For instance, 'I had a contracts professor who wrote a book on gender-neutral contracts,'" says Campbell. A student could use something like that as a way of saying what she herself is interested in. Red flag: If you find that all you and the interviewer are talking about is law school, "start paddling for shore," says Rossman.

What do you do in your spare time?

"Since starting law school, I've spent most of my spare time tutoring middle-school students, going to the gym, and reading for pleasure."

—*NYU 1L*

"I like meeting people outside of law school. It puts life in perspective. I like to read adventure books like *The Perfect Storm*. And I like to work out—jogging, tennis, soccer, basketball."

—*BU 2L*

"Reading, playing puzzle games like *Myst* or *Riven*, or watching TV, like Discovery Channel's forensic show."

—*Rutgers-Camden 1L*

Bad

Okay, so no one expects law students to live rock star social lives, but honestly, this is just ugly. Television? Never mention it, ever, no matter how "educational" the shows you claim to watch. Computer games? Never ever ever mention them. Leave aside issues of extreme geekdom. "It says that you're a couch potato," says Jawin. Meeting people outside of law school? God help you if you don't.

Good

Tutoring is an honorable way to spend a few hours of your week. Law firms aren't looking for Mother Teresas, but firms do respect people with an altruistic spirit (that said, don't act like you're "above" law firm work). An interest in an activity like tutoring also indicates that "you can focus on something other than yourself and that you use your time constructively," says Koopersmith—and those are traits a law firm definitely values. Of course, we'd be remiss if we didn't point out that the NYU student could have turned her B answer into an A by using . . . yes, specifics. Says Rossman: "She could have tried something like 'I've enjoyed tutoring middle-school students, and for the last year, I've tutored a third-grader, and it's been terrific to watch her development in math.'"

The Bottom Line

You don't have to be healing the sick, winning IQ competitions, or playing on the women's pro golf tour (though none of that would hurt). Interviewers simply want to see that you have something positive that you're passionate about—something that makes you *you*. The NYU student's answer was perfectly good; a picture of her personality emerges—someone who can focus outside herself. Fine. Finally, here's something to ease your mind: Flesher says she asks this question in part just to see how articulate people are. "I just want to know that somebody can hold an intelligent conversation. It tells me they're skilled in verbal interaction." In other words, it's a lob—sit back, relax, and show off your intelligent, verbal self.

EAT RIGHT: THE ART
OF THE RECRUITING MEAL

Okay, you aced your on-campus interviews with your favorite firm, and your formal grillings at firm headquarters have been going great. Next on the agenda: lunch or dinner with an associate. Slam dunk, right? It's just an associate—not a recruiting director or a partner. He or she may well have gone to your school. Heck, it's only a meal, not a "real" interview. All you have to do is press the flesh and down that sea bass with mango chutney. And it's not like you don't know the difference between the American and Continental methods of handling your silverware. Oh . . . you don't? Oops.

To help you dine with maximum savoir faire, *Jungle* staged a mock recruiting lunch at one of New York's finest French restaurants, La Caravelle. The players: two real-life law students (NYU 3Ls Saira Rao and Scott Winter), one real-life law firm associate (Paul Murphy, a fifth-year at New York's White & Case and a recruiting-lunch veteran), and one renowned good-manners guru (Hilka Klinkenberg, founder of Etiquette International, a consulting firm whose clients include corporate giants like American Express and Merrill Lynch). The idea? Rao and Winter acted as they would at a real recruiting lunch, and Murphy and Klinkenberg evaluated their performance.

Does etiquette matter? You bet your bonus it does. It shows you care enough about getting the job to treat the situation seriously. It shows you have the good judgment to behave in a way that's appropriate to a given situation. And it shows worldliness and sophistication.

Our posse gathered at La Caravelle on a Thursday afternoon. Over the course of an hour and a half, Rao and Winter encountered all of the usual greeting, ordering, and eating challenges. Some of what Klinkenberg saw pleased her; some did not. So that you might someday be spared an embarrassing fork faux pas, here is her critique.

Lunch Begins on the Sidewalk

The interview starts before you enter the restaurant, says Klinkenberg. "First impressions are made in a nanosecond and often form the basis of lasting conclusions." Winter entered the restaurant tucking in his shirt and adjusting his belt. Primp outside.

Dress for the Room

If you're having lunch at a fancy restaurant, dress fancy. Both students erred here, says Klinkenberg. Rao wore open-toed shoes, and Winter appeared sans tie. The restaurant's dress code trumps the firm's dress code, as well as your own, Klinkenberg says. If you can't get the name of the restaurant to research the appropriate attire, err on the side of caution and dress up, not down.

Eyes Ahead, Hand Out

Rao introduced herself to Murphy, offered a firm handshake, and looked him in the eye. Winter kept his left hand in his pocket and mumbled. Guess who Klinkenberg liked.

No, After You

Once the maître d' takes you to your table, wait for the associate to tell you where and when to sit. "If he doesn't indicate a position, ask, 'Shall I sit here?'" says Klinkenberg. As for timing, sit when he sits.

Stay Dry

When the waiter asked if anyone would like a cocktail, Rao ordered a Diet Coke, and Winter stuck with water. Good call. Even when your host indulges, avoid the booze, says Klinkenberg. "Sometimes interviewers like to throw little curveballs. He may end up taking one sip during the course of the meal."

Keep Still

Rao carried the conversation early and got points from Klinkenberg for asking thoughtful, engaging questions. But Klinkenberg noticed that she also moved her hands a lot. It's natural to be nervous, says Klinkenberg, but constant gesturing is distracting. "It's not an indication of somebody who's a professional and in command." When you're not eating, keep your hands in your lap.

When You Do Gesture, Gesture Like You Mean It

The previous item notwithstanding, gestures can be good for emphasis. When you make one, make it big. Think Bill Clinton's jabbing fist. (Try not to spill anything.)

Make the Price Right

Winter ordered the Dover sole, one of the most expensive items on the menu. Without guidance ("You must try the sole"), stick to the midrange entrées, Klinkenberg says. Going high can make you look haughty and careless with money. Going low can make you look wimpy and cheap. What if your host says, "Please, order whatever you like"? Klinkenberg still wouldn't order from the top of the price range. It could be another trap, she says.

Foie What?

If you don't understand the menu, speak up. "No one will fault you for asking questions," says Klinkenberg. "They'll fault you for looking dumb or panicked or trying to fake it." What should you say? Request suggestions, as Rao did. Try something like, "I'd like to have some fish today. What do you recommend?"

Napkin 101

Spread your napkin on your lap. Take the two corners farthest away from you, lift them up, and fold one-third of the napkin back toward you—over (not under) the rest of the napkin. To blot your mouth (always blot, never wipe), lift the underside of the folded third to your face, blot away, then return the napkin to its previous position. Food stains and lipstick smudges will be discreetly hidden from view. Slick, huh?

"Something to Start?"

If you'd like an appetizer, go ahead. Just keep it simple and relatively inexpensive.

Bread Management

Klinkenberg points out that a crumb-covered table can be prevented simply by tearing your rosemary roll over your bread plate. Sometimes, though, crumbs happen. "Leave them on the table," says Klinkenberg. Any waiter worth his tip will sweep up between courses.

"May We Recommend a Bottle of Shut Up?"

If you don't know a Chardonnay from a Chablis, don't worry: Your host will likely make the decision. If the waiter hands you a wine list, defer with grace ("I'll let my host choose"). What if you happen to know lots about the Rhône varietals of the Santa Ynez Valley? "Don't grandstand," says Klinkenberg.

Continental Versus American

Either style of utensil usage is acceptable. Continental: Keep knife and fork in the same hands at all times when cutting and eating. When resting, put both items down. American: Cut your food with your fork in your "bad" hand and your knife in your "good" hand, then put your knife on the plate and switch the fork to your opposite hand to eat. The unused hand remains in the lap. Mixing styles is a grave mistake.

No Fuss, No Muss

Rao ordered the soft-shell crab—a dangerous dish in Klinkenberg's book. Salads, soups, sandwiches, and garlic dishes should all be viewed with extreme prejudice, she says. "Choose something easy to eat."

Steak Too Tough?

Too bad, says Klinkenberg. "A business meal is never about the food. If it isn't quite to your liking, tough tiddlywinks."

Steak Still Mooing?

If a beef, chicken, or fish dish is dangerously underdone, politely call the waiter over and send it back. A good thing to say, according to Klinkenberg: "Excuse me, could this be a bit more well-done, please?" A bad thing to say: "Jeez, it looks like you just killed this thing!"

Sit Up, Lean In

Rao had good posture early, but she started to hunch over when the food arrived. Klinkenberg quickly spotted the cause: "She was sitting too far from the table." When eating, do as Winter did: Bring your chair as close to the table as possible, then lean forward with a straight back and raise the food to your mouth, directly over your plate.

"Plah Lerk Humpt"

If you're asked a question while chewing the porterhouse, "take your time and clear your mouth," says Klinkenberg (something Winter and Rao both did well). "When you get really good, you can tuck your food in the back of your mouth and talk. But that's not for amateurs." In the meantime, take smaller bites.

Return to Sender

How do you handle an olive pit or a piece of gristle in your mouth? "It comes out the way it went in," says Klinkenberg. Meaning: Remove olive pits with your fingers, gristle with your fork, and so on. And be discreet. Turn to one side, shield your mouth with your free hand, and put the offending item somewhere out of view on the plate. Look for the lettuce.

Napkin 201

If you need to get up, put your napkin on your chair, not the table. "For God's sake, don't make everyone look at a soiled napkin," says Klinkenberg.

Butterfingers!

So your cucumber/soy dipping sauce ends up on the associate's lap. Don't make a big deal about it, says Klinkenberg. "Apologize, offer to pay the cleaning bill and offer your napkin, or call the waiter." Whatever you do, "handle it quickly, discreetly, and with a minimum of fuss."

No Elbows

"Stable Mable, if you're able, keep your elbows off the table." (Rao was a repeat offender here.) While you're at it, keep your legs straight and under the table, too.

Pace Yourself

Winter cleaned his plate early. Rao had barely made a dent in hers well after the others had finished. "Pay attention to the speed of the meal," says Klinkenberg. If you're getting ahead of the others, slow down. If you're falling behind, ask questions to buy yourself some eating time. If you find that everyone else is done but you still have a long way to go, says Klinkenberg, "stop. You're finished, too."

Doggie Bag?

You're kidding, right? Yeah, we thought so.

What to Do
When You're Done

When she was finished eating, Rao laid her knife and fork willy-nilly across her plate. Wrong. Imagine your plate is a clock. Place the silver at four o'clock.

"The Bill, Monsieur"

If the waiter puts the check in front of you, be cool. "Just leave it. It's not yours to look at," says Klinkenberg. He who invites pays.

Finish With Style

Thank-yous are always welcome, but keep them short and sweet. Klinkenberg has no advice for how to tidy up a brown nose.

ETIQUETTE

It's not just what you say in an interview. It's also how you look and act. Here, the *Jungle* guide.

1. Shower, comb hair, trim nails, apply deodorant/ antiperspirant, brush teeth. Perfume or cologne? Sure, but just a little. Altoids? Definitely. Have two.
2. Men: solid or pin-striped blue or gray suit; solid blue or white shirt; simple, classic tie; black or brown shoes in excellent condition, spit-polished. Shirt collar should be snug but not tight, shirtsleeves should extend one thumb's width below jacket sleeves, and pants should "break" at the shoe. Socks should match pants, not shoes. Belt should match shoes, not pants.
3. Women: Wear a suit (pants are okay) but nothing extreme. No Ally McBeal–length skirts or Manolo Blahnik spiked heels. No low-cut shirts or tops, no lacey camisoles. Accessorize minimally. In general, think J.Crew, not J.Lo.
4. Men and women: If it's cold or raining, get yourself a proper overcoat and a good umbrella. A coat with

The North Face on it is not proper. An umbrella with Lancôme on it is not good.

5. Galoshes? Definitely. And while you're at it, print the letters d-o-r-k on them.

6. Just before meeting the interviewer, wipe the sweat off your palms. Do this well out of her sight.

7. When you meet the interviewer, look her in the eye and give her a firm handshake. Note: "Look her in the eye" does not mean "Stare into her soul and freak her out." "Firm" does not mean bone-crushing.

8. Don't be late.

9. Ever.

10. If something happens that forces you to be late, explain the lateness (quickly), apologize (once), and move on (fast).

11. Carry a pen, notebook, extra resumés, and transcripts.

12. When fielding and answering questions, maintain eye contact with your interviewer, sit up straight, and don't fidget. If you're stumped for an answer, look down—it communicates thoughtfulness.

13. Be enthusiastic but not too enthusiastic. Recruiters are pros at sniffing out BS.

14. Smile, but don't be a grinning dolt. Appear pleasant yet serious.

15. Be concise.

16. Your fly is zipped, isn't it? Your cell phone is off, yes? You have a hanky in your pocket in case you sneeze, don't you? You know that sneezes sometimes produce a visible mess, right?

17. If an interviewer asks you a question about your age, religion, child-rearing plans, sexual orientation, or anything else illegal or inappropriate, politely say, "That doesn't seem relevant to my ability to work here. Perhaps there's something job-related you'd like to ask me."

18. When saying good-bye to an interviewer, acceptable phrases include: (a) "I enjoyed meeting you. I look forward to hearing from you"; (b) "That was a pleasure—thank you for taking the time"; (c) "Please let me know if there's anything else you need from me."

19. When saying good-bye to an interviewer, unacceptable phrases include: (a) "Dude, that was awesome! Later!"; (b) "So, did I get the job? Well, did I?"; (c) "Did you know the human head weighs eight pounds?"

20. Thank-you notes? Yes. Form letters? Sure—deliver them in your galoshes.

CLERKSHIPS

After Debra Strauss graduated from Yale Law School, she clerked for the former chief judge of the Southern District of New York. "It was the best professional experience of my life, without question," says Strauss, adjunct professor and codirector of Pace University School of Law's clerkship program and author of *Behind the Bench: The Guide to Judicial Clerkships* (BarBri Group, 2002).

If you are considering a clerkship, make sure that you enjoy legal research, writing, editing, and cite-checking. While duties vary, clerks often draft bench memoranda and judicial decisions; they sometimes also help judges draft speeches and journal articles. Clerks may also maintain libraries, collect documents, and assist with docketing.

Why consider clerking? In addition to being excellent learning experiences, clerkships are also prestigious. Many respected attorneys and law school professors, including four current Supreme Court justices, are former clerks. Also, clerkships can often open the door to plum jobs, and many firms and organizations grant former clerks seniority status on the path to partnership and in the salary pool, not to mention hefty signing bonuses.

Clerks also have the opportunity to work closely with people who are already experienced, knowledgeable, and distinguished in their careers. Strauss, who formerly directed her alma mater's judicial clerkship program, still keeps in touch with the judge for whom she clerked when she graduated—and to whom she later returned as a "permanent" law clerk. "You have a lifelong mentor who is a judge," she says. "He really opened up the world of the judiciary to me."

Applying for a Clerkship

Many students and lawyers hoping to clerk apply to a large number of judges, as the process is extremely competitive. Clerkships in a federal court or the highest state courts are generally seen as the most prestigious—and therefore the most difficult to land. Keep in mind also that popular circuits and cities receive more applications than others. Yet clerkship opportunities abound in trial and appellate courts at the state and federal levels; in federal specialty courts, such as the United States Tax Court; and with federal bankruptcy court, magistrate, or administrative law judges.

"You have to be flexible as to courts and judges, and even as to types of clerkships," Strauss advises. "The farther you go off the beaten path, the higher your chances are of getting a clerkship."

Good grades will carry you far in the application process; other important resumé items include honors like law review. A judicial internship or externship can also boost your chances of landing a clerkship. A favorable recommendation from a judge can go a long way, as "word of mouth is really a great entrée into the judicial system," says Strauss.

Judges are very interested in potential clerks' writing abilities, says Strauss. She advises applicants to seek recommendations from professors who are familiar with their writing skills and to tailor their writing samples to the courts. District court applications, for example, should include a piece of "concrete legal writing," whereas an applicant to a court of appeals might either select a more theoretical piece or also include a brief or memorandum. Strauss adds that applicants should introduce their writing with a relevant explanation.

If you're entertaining the idea of applying for a clerkship, visit your law school's career office. Your school probably offers materials describing the clerkship application process and timelines. Career counselors can offer advice as well as connect you with alumni and faculty members willing to discuss their clerkship experiences. They may also be able to point you toward information sessions you should attend. You may also wish to research the backgrounds of the judges to whom you are sending applications.

Be aware of the deadlines for submitting clerkship applications. Federal appellate judges recently voted to postpone hiring law clerks until the 3L fall semester. Other judges maintain different hiring timetables, and students may apply for clerkships through their third year for positions that will begin shortly after graduation or at a later date. "Check with each judge," Strauss cautions, and be ready with your applications. She also advises applicants to take the first interview slot a judge offers, since "the position may not be there a day later."

If you must travel far for an interview, you may wish to call other local judges to whom you applied to see if they are interested in interviewing you while you're in the area. Finally, Strauss notes that it is customary not to turn down an offer from a judge. You might have a small window of time in which to consider an offer (and call other judges with whom you interviewed to see if they intend to select you), but if you do not have another offer, think twice before saying no: Rejecting a judge's offer may leave you excluded from certain chambers— and you might also jeopardize your classmates' chances of securing a clerkship.

Unfortunately, law schools outside the top 10 don't always do enough to encourage their students to clerk. If your school doesn't produce many clerks, that may be because few of its graduates apply. If you want a clerkship, go for it.

SUMMER ASSOCIATE WISDOM

Come summer, thousands of students start their careers at law firms as summer associates. How can you be the best summer associate possible? *JD Jungle* held roundtable panels at two of the country's top law firms—Vinson & Elkins, in Dallas, and Weil, Gotshal & Manges, in New York—and asked the participants to reveal the secrets of first-year associate success. Their advice is useful for summer associates as well.

THE ADVISERS

Vinson & Elkins
Jeffrey Chapman, Managing Partner
Rob Walters, Managing Partner
Randy Jurgensmeyer, Transactions Partner
Jim Meyer, Hiring Partner
Weil, Gotshal & Manges
Mark Hoenig, Tax Partner
David Lender, Litigation Partner
Vickie Germain Kobak,
    Director of Professional Development
Brad Scott, Director of Associate Relations

Blast the Past

"Leave your credentials at the door," says Vinson & Elkins' Rob Walters. "What you did in law school no longer matters."

Steel Yourself

"Expect to encounter real challenges," says V&E's Jeffrey Chapman. "It may sound obvious, but law firm work is difficult. Just accepting that can make things easier."

Listen Good

At your first meeting with a partner, it's not necessary to say or do anything brilliant. It is necessary to understand your instructions. "A mistake a lot of people make is walking out of my office without knowing what I want," says Weil's Mark Hoenig. "As eager as you are to look smart, and as busy as I might be, don't walk away without knowing what I said." Take notes and ask questions, Hoenig advises. "When you leave, say things like: 'I hear what you're saying. I know what you want. I'll get right on it.' It gives me confidence that you understand."

Follow Up

After the first meeting, says Hoenig, put as much energy as you can, as quickly as you can, into taking care of whatever matter you were asked to address. Then go back to the partner quickly—so quickly that he knows you can't possibly have the full answer yet—and tell him you want to bounce a few ideas off of him. "He'll see you've been busting your butt," says Hoenig. "He'll know you heard what he was saying. He'll see that you're thinking and exploring. And you'll get the benefit of having him tell you where to go next."

Think Positive

"New associates often get assignments they consider boring," says Weil's Vickie Germain Kobak. It's easy to complain, but associates who get ahead approach such work with a positive attitude, she says. Recognize that so-called scut work often proves useful later. "If you do due diligence, for example, you learn how a company works. That might help in the future when you do an acquisition or a divestiture." And ask your supervisor how your task relates to the case or transaction as a whole: "You'll feel connected to the larger cause," says Germain Kobak. And don't forget: "A law firm is a team. The work has to get done. Everyone has to take his turn."

Stick to It

"There's always a way to get out of an assignment," says Weil's David Lender. "But I think a smarter approach is to grin and bear it. I've always noticed that the people who show initiative and work hard somehow get connected to the best people and cases."

Do the Time

"Look around and see how busy your peers are," says V&E's Randy Jurgensmeyer. "If you're working a lot harder, take that into account. If you're not working as much as they are, get yourself more work."

Don't Be Perfect

A lot of young associates are perfectionists, says Jurgensmeyer. "They will work and work on, say, researching a memo and won't want to let it go until it's perfect." Instead of searching for perfection, aim to develop a sense of cost versus benefit. "Will more work yield a meaningful improvement? If so, keep working. If not, stop." Follow the old saw "Don't let the perfect be the enemy of the good."

Do Be Perfect

"Young lawyers often are not trained to be thorough and precise," says V&E's Chapman. "Their law school exams involved throwing as much intellectual stuff on the wall as they could." But in the real world, says Chapman, "sweat the details. The details matter enormously."

Hit the Deadline

"It's a fundamental law of firm life," says Chapman. "If somebody you're working for needs something at a certain time, get it to him."

Sound Alarms Early

If you must miss a deadline, "give me the heads-up early," says Jurgensmeyer. "Nobody likes surprises. Say 'I've got a real problem and this just isn't going to work out.' As long as you don't do it often, and as long as you give me enough time to find a solution, it shouldn't be a big deal."

Cross the T's

"Something I find extremely annoying," says Walters, "is when somebody gives me a document and says 'It's not really finished, but I know you're going to revise it, so I'm giving it to you anyway.' That's just like missing a deadline."

Never, Ever Bluff

"It's okay not to know the answer," says Chapman. "But don't bluff. If you don't know, say you don't know. Tell them you'll find out and get back to them. Bluffing only leads to bigger problems."

'Fess Up If You Foul Up

"Don't try to hide mistakes," says Jurgensmeyer. "Tell us now what they are. If you hide them, you'll get into trouble down the road. The most important thing you have is your reputation. If you lose that, you're in trouble."

Get Yourself a Guru

"The important thing about a mentor relationship is the chemistry," says Weil's Brad Scott. "Even if your firm has a formal mentoring program, seek your own advisers within the firm. Informal relationships often work best."

Dress Like a Pro

Says Germain Kobak, the question to ask is "Do I look professional? Am I the kind of person clients or partners want representing them—as opposed to the person they want to sit and watch TV with or the person they want to ask on a date?"

Stay Off TV

When composing e-mail, "use the Mike Wallace Test," says Walters. "If you could stand getting grilled by Wallace about the message, go ahead and write it. If not, don't."

Be Yourself, Stupid

"When you get to a law firm, you're working with a lot of smart people and a lot of resources, and you're no longer allowed to send out a letter without showing it to somebody. There's a tendency to look at all that and to forget what you're made of," says Hoenig. "If you're not careful, you can lose your sense of who you are and what you're capable of. Once you stop feeling that, you stop thinking and you start reacting. And once you go down that slide, you're lost."

Be Like This Guy

"I'll paint you a picture of the type of associate I like," says Hoenig. "He works long hours, he tries, he takes the initiative, he always comes back to me with ideas, he never says he has researched something that he hasn't. He makes my life easy, and I can trust him. Think about that."

Finally, Think About All This . . .

- "The most important characteristics you need are perseverance and an eye for detail," says Jurgens-meyer.
- "A law firm job is what you make of it," says Scott.
- "If you don't understand, ask," says Germain Kobak.
- "When I was an associate, my attitude was basically: 'You want me to wash the windows? I'll wash the windows,'" says Lender.
- "Be the person that others want to turn to," says Walters.
- "If you compromise your integrity, it's like ripping open a pillow and trying to gather the feathers—you will never get it back," says Chapman.
- "New associates tend to think of a law firm as an institution. It's not. It's just people. Make your personal relationships work," says Hoenig. "That's the code to crack."

SUMMER ASSOCIATE DON'TS

Ah, the summer associate job—the critical first step in what you hope will be a long, profitable, and noble legal career. So what do you do? You destroy partners' prized possessions, relieve (and expose) yourself in front of colleagues, and hit on your superiors' wives. Below, a roundup of real-life summer associate screwups. Names have been omitted and identifying details have been changed to protect . . . you'll see.

The Golf Pro

A top New York City law firm held its annual golf outing at a posh country club. Summer associates were invited, and one—a nongolfer—was particularly nervous about having to play. Naturally, he was called on to tee off first—in front of the clubhouse, in full view of everyone. Sure enough, he duck-hooked his tee shot straight into the parking lot. But wait—that's not all. The ball flew smack into the windshield of a vintage Porsche owned by one of the firm's senior partners, smashing the glass to bits.

The Ladies' Man

A partner from a New York City firm hosted a summer associate dinner at his house, a lovely brownstone on the city's Upper West Side. Everyone was having a fine time, including one attractive, flirtatious male associate who spent more than an hour chatting up a beautiful woman. As the conversation ended, the associate asked the woman if she'd like to get together sometime. She thanked him, said no, then politely informed him that she was the host partner's wife. His shocked response: "Yeah, I know."

The Dancing Fool

After a company dinner, a group of summer associates and a few lawyers from a white-shoe New York City firm decided to take a few spins around the dance floor at the ultratony Rainbow Room. One summer associate, a tall, attractive blonde, had claimed to be quite the dancer, and she soon joined a male partner on the dance floor. Before long the partner twirled the young woman away from him, and as she spun back toward him, the self-styled Ginger Rogers swung her arm through the air and smacked her Fred Astaire dead in the mouth, loosening a tooth. Fred was taken to an emergency dentist; Ginger was left to wallow in embarrassment.

The Drunken Sailor

One of San Francisco's larger firms hosts an annual boat excursion around San Francisco Bay. Having spent the better part of the outing availing himself of certain cold beverages, one young associate suddenly found himself in need of a men's room. For reasons unknown, our man shunned the standard facilities and relieved himself over the side of the boat—in full view of his shipmates. Later, in a bid to reveal as many body parts to as many people as possible, he mooned the passengers of another craft.

The Sensitive Type

Already facing several strikes for bad behavior, a male associate at a large Boston firm was working late one night with a female lawyer. After talking for a while, the associate apparently felt comfortable enough with his coworker to share some of his personal aspirations. In particular, he listed the women at the firm he wanted to sleep with. The next day, the woman complained to a group of partners, and when the perp was asked about the incident, he confirmed that it was, in fact, true. One partner then relayed the coworker's anger and dismay and asked the man whether he understood why the woman in question was upset. His response: "Because I left her off my list?"

The Fallout

What became of our heroes?
The Golf Pro: Received and accepted an offer at the firm.
The Ladies' Man: No offer.
The Dancing Fool: Took a clerkship after law school.
The Drunken Sailor: No offer.
The Sensitive Type: Fired.

The Third Year: Relax

- Academics
- Extracurriculars
- Jobs
- Good-bye

YOUR THIRD YEAR IS THE LAST BIT OF FREEDOM YOU'LL HAVE BEFORE YOU TAKE THE PLUNGE INTO THE PRACTICE OF LAW (OR WHATEVER CAREER YOU CHOOSE). BUT IT'S POINTLESS TO PAY A FORTUNE IN TUITION just to twiddle your thumbs. Here's how to make the most of a year that's known more for being a waste of time than a rite of passage.

ACADEMICS

By the time your third year rolls around, whatever terror accompanied 1L courses will be a distant memory. "Expect to be challenged, not tortured" in your last year, says Heather Parker, a 2000 graduate of the John Marshall Law School in Atlanta. "You can now absorb information much more easily and rapidly."

You may find that the real difficulty lies not in staying up to speed in your classes but in simply staying motivated. If your 2L summer went as planned, you will probably have your post-graduation job lined up already. As long as you don't flunk out, your offer is safe. So unless you're in the running for a degree with honors (and you care about making it), grades are just as irrelevant as they were during the spring of your senior year in high school.

Because the pressure is off, you finally have the opportunity to study what you like and to learn for learning's sake. "You are going to learn what you need to know for the bar when you take the [bar review] class over the summer, so choose classes that truly interest you and that you have wanted to take since you got to school," says a New York University 3L. Chances are, this is it for your academic career, so don't miss the chance to try a course in a new field.

EXTRACURRICULARS

If you'd rather not use this year to catch up on sleep, focus on extracurriculars. "I've worked more this year than I have in years past, but that is entirely because of my activities," says David, a Harvard 3L.

While extracurriculars may become more intense as graduation approaches, you may also find that the nature of the work changes in positive ways. Third-year students usually run the show at journals; 2Ls are stuck with the scut work. Take the opportunity to develop your leadership skills and mentor 2Ls as they learn the ropes at your organization.

JOBS

If you end up without a tempting offer after your 2L summer, the job hunt will dominate your 3L experience. "The earlier you find a job, the less hectic third year will be," says Kevin, a student at the Washington College of Law at American University. Even if you have an offer from a firm, you might want to defer it to apply for a public-interest fellowship or other special program. "Looking for jobs didn't help [make third year any easier]," says David, who explored public-service options despite having an offer from a prestigious firm. "I tried (and failed) to get a fellowship; that was very busy and stressful."

If your school provides services to make the process easier, take advantage of whatever help is available. "Be sure to make use of all that your school has to offer in the way of career services and mock-interviewing sessions," Parker says.

> TIP: Since personal contacts are key to finding jobs outside of the organized interview process, attend as many networking events as possible.

Remember that your first job is only that—a first job—and that greater opportunities may present themselves after you've spent a year in the market.

SAYING GOOD-BYE

While most 3Ls say that they feel ready to move on, they also encourage their 2L counterparts to enjoy the freedom of their last year in school. "Take advantage of it, make plans to see people you don't always get to see, explore the city you live in, pursue hobbies or things you have been wanting to try—if it's there and I can't see it because your schedule will never be this flexible again," advises an NYU 3L. You may also feel that your final year is whizzing by much more quickly than the previous two. "I did actually start to see the light at the end of the tunnel," says Parker. "Your third year will be over before you know it."

After three years of bonding with your classmates, saying good-bye may be one of the toughest challenges of the year. "I have met lots of great people at law school, and many of them are good friends who I will miss," says Robert, a Harvard 3L. Hopefully, you'll feel the same way about your class after you've been scared, worked, and bored to death together. Stay in touch with your classmates after graduation; after all, no one else will understand what you've been through.

Behind the Bar

• •

- Frequently Asked Questions
- How to Prepare
- The Biggest, Baddest Bar

BAR EXAMS RANK SOMEWHERE NEAR ROOT CANALS ON THE LIST OF THINGS YOU WISH YOU NEVER HAD TO GO THROUGH. ASK ANY LAWYER TO RELIVE THE EXPERIENCE AND YOU'LL PROBABLY GET A RESPONSE like that of one second-year associate at a Washington, D.C., firm: "It's the only thing you'll ever have to do that's actually *worse* than everything you've heard about it."

A tad dramatic? Richard Conviser, a graduate of the University of California–Berkeley's Boalt Hall School of Law and veteran professor at Chicago's ITT/Kent Law School, doesn't think so. That's why, more than 30 years ago, he founded the Bar Review Institute (which became the ubiquitous BAR/BRI when it merged with Bay Area Review in 1974) to provide lawyers-to-be with a knowledgeable guide through this Scylla and Charybdis of tests. As Conviser points out, the pool of bar-takers is already highly qualified: They have graduated from college, scored well on the LSAT, been accepted to law school, and completed three years of intense academic study. So it only makes sense that the bar exam should outdo all of the above challenges and serve as a final separator of the attorneys from the also-rans.

ANSWERS TO FREQUENTLY ASKED QUESTIONS

Why do I have to take it?

Since the quality of education and specific curricula vary significantly from school to school, the bar exam determines a standard level of competency among law school graduates. In conjunction with a demonstration of sufficient character and fitness (your bar application includes a questionnaire used to determine that you are "worthy of the trust and confidence clients may reasonably place in their lawyers"), a passing score on the bar exam allows you to become a lawyer in the state of your choice.

Massachusetts administered the first written bar exam in 1855. Until that point, the exams had been administered orally. Bar exams continued to become increasingly formal and regulated, and in 1931 the National Conference of Bar Examiners (NCBE) was established to help "develop, maintain, and apply reasonable and uniform standards of education and character for eligibility for admission to the practice of law."

What is it?

Unlike the LSAT, which measures your logical and analytical skills, this test is strictly knowledge-based. Another difference between the bar and the LSAT: This exam is one you can actually *fail*. It's essentially a 25- to 30-subject final exam on all the classes you've taken in law school—including stuff you haven't seen since your first year—as well as some subjects that you may have never covered in a classroom. As you might imagine, studying for this exam is not optional: It's just as much a rite of passage as taking the exam itself.

Each state designs and administers its own exam for admission to its bar, drawing on a combination of four NCBE-sponsored standardized tests: the Multistate Professional Responsibility Exam (MPRE), the Multistate Bar Exam (MBE), the Multistate Essay Exam (MEE), and the Multistate Performance Test (MPT). In addition, individual jurisdictions can develop their own local exams that address their specific laws and exceptions. These tests are usually in an essay format, but some states, like Florida, also use multiple-choice questions.

Who can take it?

You must qualify to sit for the bar exam, which usually means graduating from an American Bar Association–approved law school. Some jurisdictions also allow other means of qualification, such as one year of law school study and apprenticeship at a law firm for a certain period. (Fun fact: Abraham Lincoln—one of the most respected lawyers in U.S. history—never attended law school and even went on to become a bar examiner.)

When do I take it?

All jurisdictions using the standardized one-day MBE (only Louisiana, Washington State, and Puerto Rico do not) are required to administer the test on the last Wednesdays in July and February each year. The remainder of a state's bar admissions testing takes place either on the Tuesday immediately prior, the Thursday immediately following, or both.

While most students take the bar exam in July, students who want to take it in a second state, who graduate in the fall, or who didn't pass their first time around can take it in February.

Which state should I choose?

For dyed-in-the-wool Texans whose roots run deeper than the family oil well, this one's a no-brainer. If, however, you grew up in Connecticut, attended school in both Pennsylvania and Virginia, are moving to D.C. after law school, and plan to end up in New York City someday, your decision might not be so cut-and-dried.

This was the case for one JD from the University of Virginia. He ultimately decided to take the bar exam in two states—New York and Connecticut—and then take advantage of the District of Columbia's waive-in policy (see below) so that he could practice at a firm there.

Some states are particularly accommodating to lawyers who need to practice in multiple states simultaneously or switch from state to neighboring state, and they have set up their exam schedules accordingly so candidates can test in just one three-day session rather than several separate ones. For example, the New York bar recognizes that it will often share lawyers with surrounding states and has made it easy for candidates to take its exam concurrently with New Jersey, Maryland, Massachusetts, Maine, or Connecticut.

In other states, like California—long reputed to have one of the most difficult examinations in the country because of its length as well as its low passing rate (55.3 percent for the July 2000 exam)—you won't have the option to take more than one state test per administration. California's exam runs three days, so if you want to be licensed to practice elsewhere at the same time, you may have to hit the books twice.

There are places, though—like Washington, D.C.—that have very liberal reciprocity rules; some will allow a lawyer who has passed the bar in another jurisdiction to waive in to their own—in other words, to apply for eligibility to practice in their state without having to take another bar.

Different states have different levels of reciprocity. The District of Columbia requires only that candidates be bar-certified elsewhere and that they have a sponsoring lawyer based in Washington to vouch for their competence and professionalism; many states require that candidates have been bar-certified elsewhere for three or more years before applying. Some states refuse to let anyone waive in at all. Florida is one: In order to practice law in the Sunshine State, you must pass its bar exam. Period. (Perhaps this is intended to discourage snow-weary northern lawyers from trying to retire early to Palm Beach!)

As you choose the bar that's best for you, consider three main issues: where you'd like to practice immediately after graduation, whether you might transfer within your firm to offices in other states, and where you'd ultimately like to settle down.

Pamela, a student at Georgetown University with a job waiting for her at Baker & McKenzie in Washington, D.C., plans to take the New York bar exam. It's one of the most respected in the country, so it's not too difficult to waive in to other states. (Check with your state's bar admissions office to see which reciprocity rules apply to you.) Also, because the Big Apple is the hub of most corporate transactions, it's a good exam to take if you're interested, as Pamela is, in corporate law.

Once you determine the state (or states) in which you'd like to practice, you'll have to learn the nuances of their specific bar exams. Because each state is allowed to determine the makeup of its test, exams vary in their level of difficulty. Whereas the MBE is standard throughout most of the country, the material tested on the rest of the days is left up to each state's discretion.

New York's bar exam, while only two days long, is considered one of the hardest in the country. Not only does New York have many exceptions to the general law; its state-specific essay questions also cover combinations of 27 different areas of law—often asking candidates to draw upon several areas of knowledge to answer each question. States with three-day exams, like California and Texas, require more work as well as more endurance from candidates.

Virginia's bar exam is deemed even more difficult because it not only tests candidates on 28 different subjects but also requires in-depth knowledge of minority law that often contradicts the rules you need to study for the multistate exam. Consequently, Virginia has one of the lowest pass rates in the country. Even worse, you can't sport those lucky sweats that got you through the LSAT: The conservative state requires that its aspiring lawyers take the bar in attire "suitable for a lawyer appearing in a court of record" (yes, that means a suit). Interestingly, it also mandates wearing soft-soled shoes to minimize noise in the testing rooms. The result: a room full of stressed-out fashion victims wearing suits and sneakers.

Where is it administered?

Exams are usually administered on university campuses, in convention centers, or in hotel conference rooms. Some test-takers get luckier than others. One New York bar veteran fondly remembers taking the test at a museum in Albany with a phenomenal view of the Adirondacks. (He does note, however, that this was "the only 'pretty' part of the experience.") One veteran suffered through the deafening noise of an equipment sound check for a concert that was being held outside his testing site on the second day of the exam. He recounts, "I could barely hear myself think. The woman next to me started crying. One guy just threw his hands up and walked out." The moral of the story? Be prepared for anything.

How do I register for the bar exam?

Registration deadlines for both the February and July exams are usually from 90 to 120 days before the testing date. Some states, like California, offer online registration. Regular-deadline registration fees vary but start at about $100 and may run as high as $1,000 (in those states with more labor-intensive testing, such as hand-graded MPTs). Late registration can tack on a significant amount to the already steep prices, so save a few hundred dollars and don't put this one off.

How is the exam structured?

With a few exceptions (like the aforementioned California and Texas), most states' bar exams consist of two days of testing: the Wednesday MBE, and a Tuesday or Thursday state-specific exam.

The MBE

The MBE covers the areas of legal knowledge that all lawyers should have mastered and is often considered the most significant component of the exam. Its 200 multiple-choice questions are broken up into two three-hour sections—one administered in the morning, one in the afternoon.

Questions are conceived by committees of lawyers and law professors and then reviewed and edited by several legal experts and psychometricians. They cover six different subject areas, most of which were addressed in your first year of law school: constitutional law, contracts, criminal law and procedure, evidence, real property, and torts. The majority of the questions test your knowledge of general legal principles, but some will provide statutes or exceptions for you to consider when formulating your answer. Because no points are taken off for wrong answers, *answer every question*. You'll most likely have plenty of time to finish: Statistics show that the three-hour time frame for each set of 100 questions is sufficient for 99 percent of all test-takers.

The MBE is the only portion of the bar exam where scoring is centralized and consistent across the country. Your raw score is the number of questions you answered correctly out of a possible 200. In addition to your raw score, however, the NCBE will also report a scaled score that adjusts for variations in the difficulty of your particular exam.

States differ on how heavily they weight MBE performance in the overall score. In most states it makes up about half the total, but South Carolina, for example, only counts it for one-seventh. Though passing requirements vary from state to state, they generally hover around the 130–140 scaled-score range. Nationwide, around 60–80 percent of applicants pass the MBE.

Local Tests

The local portion of each exam generally comprises a series of essay questions on the laws and their exceptions in the specific state. These essay questions give prospective lawyers the opportunity to demonstrate their ability to reason, analyze, and communicate their conclusions given a set of circumstances within the constraints of state law. In most states, this requires another six-hour day of testing.

Some states also use the NCBE-sponsored MEE and MPT as part of their local testing.

The MEE

Only 14 jurisdictions, including Hawaii, Missouri, and the District of Columbia, use the MEE as part of their state-specific essay-question section. Though it's a standardized test, the MEE is scored and evaluated by the state in which it is administered rather than by a central scoring agency. The three-hour exam is made up of six essay questions covering agency and partnership, commercial paper, conflict of laws, corporations, decedents' estates, family law, federal civil procedure, sales, secured transactions, and trusts and future interests. It is administered on the Tuesday before the last Wednesday of February and July.

The MPT

Many states, from Alaska to West Virginia, also include one or more of the three 90-minute items in the MPT in their state-specific day of testing. And more and more are joining their ranks. The exam is administered on the Tuesday before and/or the Thursday after the last Wednesday in February and July.

The MPT asks candidates to use their general legal knowledge to perform practical tasks—like writing a memo or a brief—under realistic circumstances. Each MPT includes a "file" (containing a memorandum from a supervising attorney and documents that may or may not be relevant to the case) and a "library" (containing relevant and/or irrelevant cases and statutes). Although it does test some legal knowledge, it is primarily a test of the skills that you will use as a lawyer. Like the MEE, the MPT is scored locally.

The MPRE

Students usually take the MPRE in November of their third year of law school. It's also administered in March and August. You study for it separately (although most students confess that they don't spend too much time or energy preparing for it).

Essentially, this 50-question, two-hour, multiple-choice exam tests commonsense rules of professional responsibility, and it's considerably more difficult to fail than the more intensive and comprehensive bar exam. Most states have a first-time pass rate of about 90 percent. Maryland, Washington State, Wisconsin, and Puerto Rico do not require the MPRE.

The score that you receive on the MPRE will be a scaled version—between 50 and 150—of your maximum raw score and is rated according to the test's relative difficulty. Passing scores are determined by the supreme courts in each jurisdiction, so they fluctuate (generally from 75 to 85) from state to state.

While the MPRE is not part of the two- or three-day bar exam itself, a passing score is still necessary to be eligible to practice law in most jurisdictions. Regular registration deadlines are usually about five weeks before the exam date, and the registration fee is $50 (the cost doubles if you register late).

HOW TO PREPARE

Preparing for the bar exam is essential. Law firms recognize this, and most give their incoming first-year associates the summer off after graduation (sometimes salaried) to study for the late-July administration. Many firms will even pick up the tab for expensive prep courses or offer a stipend for registration and preparation expenses.

One of the biggest reasons to take a prep course is that your schooling alone will most likely not have provided you with all the information you'll need. Robert Feinberg, president and CEO of the bar review course PMBR (Professional Multistate Bar Review), asserts that "law schools don't prepare students for the bar exam"—bar-review courses prepare students for the bar exam. Pamela had no interest in tax law, so she chose not to waste a full three credits studying it. Instead, she'll get the essential information on tax law in New York—the state in which she's taking her exam—in condensed form from her BAR/BRI prep course.

Richard Conviser offers perhaps the most persuasive argument of all for not going into the bar exam less than fully prepared: "Bar exam failure has very public ramifications." If you don't pass the exam, your friends, colleagues, and—in many cases—anyone who visits your state bar's website will know about it. (If your last name is Kennedy, your less-than-stellar performance could make headlines for weeks.) And, of course, you won't be a lawyer until you do pass.

Firms are generally accommodating to first-year associates who learn in November that they have failed the bar. Especially if you've wowed them in your first three months on the job, they will usually let you stick around and retake the exam in February. Of course, your business card will only say "law clerk" until you pass. If the second time is also a no-go, many firms won't give you the chance to see if the third's a charm before they say *sayonara*.

Most states, however, will let you take the exam as many times as necessary. In 1997, 42-year-old Herbert Moreira-Brown passed the New York State bar after more than a dozen attempts. As he told the *New York Law Journal*, "If you pass it once, it doesn't matter how many times you failed."

Prep-Course Primer

If you don't adhere to Moreira-Brown's philosophy, however, sign up for a prep course—or two, or three. The biggest and most reputable name in bar review is BAR/BRI, the only nationwide course offering preparation for all 50 states' bar exams. PMBR is also a familiar name for most 3Ls; it's well known for its condensed three- and six-day MBE-only prep courses. Both have been around for over a quarter-century; both are extremely comprehensive and offer various services to students from their first semester in law school; and both carry hefty price tags—from several hundred to a couple thousand dollars each, depending on the bar (or bars) you're preparing for.

There are also "boutique" prep courses—like Fleming's Fundamentals of Law in California—and a few less-expensive at-home study programs. These courses, however, are appropriate for students only in a handful of states and are not as well-established as either BAR/BRI or PMBR.

Pamela is taking PMBR's six-day course in addition to her BAR/BRI preparation. She won't be alone. Many aspiring lawyers double up on prep courses. They want to know that they went into the exam having done absolutely everything to ensure a passing score the first time around. As the BAR/BRI T-shirt quips: "Do it right. Do it once. Never, ever do it again."

You can take BAR/BRI without taking PMBR, but you can't take PMBR alone, as it only preps you for the MBE and not the state-specific or essay portions of the exam. PMBR bills itself as a supplement to a BAR/BRI-type course, and it endorses taking both. Feinberg founded PMBR on the premise that a good score on the MBE can make up for a weaker score on the state-specific section. For example, Florida requires a combined score of 262 on both its MBE and local tests, so every point over 131 that you earn on the MBE earns you points toward your local score. In fact, there seems to be an unwritten theory among bar exam experts that, in most states, if you can ace the MBE, you'll pass the whole thing.

Many students take PMBR's short course during the two-week gap between the end of their BAR/BRI course and the exam date. Some former test-takers caution against this tactic, however, asserting that there's not enough time left to absorb all the information PMBR throws at you and that it's better to take advantage of it earlier in your study period.

One Virginia examinee didn't bother with PMBR at all, however. She knew that it would only help her with about 40 percent of her score (Virginia counts your results on its own state-specific test for 60 percent of the total) and that much of the information would in fact be contradictory to what she would need to know for her local exam.

Both BAR/BRI and PMBR have earned their stripes by hiring only currently practicing lawyers and law professors, as well as by providing students with the most up-to-date practice questions and review materials. BAR/BRI consistently researches and analyzes each state's exams in order to help students focus their study on the areas they're most likely to see on the test. For example, BAR/BRI can usually predict which combinations of New York's 27 possible essay subjects are likely to show up on the administration for which you're preparing. And if you plan to take a bar exam in more than one state, most prep courses—including BAR/BRI—will cut you a deal on the cost of double-prepping, whether you do it at the same time or in tandem.

Inside a Prep Course

BAR/BRI's lecture-style classes are led by experts in each subject. Course material is customized to each state's exam, and lessons are separated by subject, addressing both the rules and their exceptions for each specific state. This format allows you to study for both the MBE and the local test simultaneously.

Unless you're taking a class in the most popular city in the state for which you're studying, you'll watch all of your classes on videotape. Though this may seem impersonal, it's actually of little consequence whether you attend live or recorded lectures: The material itself is well-outlined in BAR/BRI's prepared guides, and even in live classes students aren't allowed to interrupt the professor with questions. Many professors do give out their direct office numbers, however, to students who view either live or recorded classes. If all else fails, you can always call BAR/BRI's question-and-answer hotline. BAR/BRI does provide live lecturers in multiple locations in all states for its one-day MPRE prep class. There are no MPRE courses on tape.

Taking a bar review course, like the one BAR/BRI offers, can be more intense than any of the classes you endured in law school. For the July exam, for example, BAR/BRI's classes begin shortly after graduation in May and run for six weeks. Each week, you can expect four or five days of lectures—about four hours each day—and three to four hours of condensing your notes. In addition, you'll have about two hours' worth of reviewing and practice questions to do on each weekday, with another eight to ten hours of work waiting for you on the weekends.

BAR/BRI advises its students to take one day off from studying each week for the first month of the course, and for good reason: Students who study nonstop for six weeks are more likely to burn out early, leaving them drained and test-weary long before the actual exam date.

Some boutique courses, like Fleming's, offer personalized tutoring as part of their course. (Fleming's tutoring package runs about $5,500.) Others, like BAR/BRI, provide individual attention in the form of a hotline. Hiring a tutor is not a complete substitute for taking a course and is not often necessary because the nuances of each state's exam are pretty cut-and-dried, but some test-takers feel more secure with personalized attention. You can often find local bar exam experts through your university's newspaper or bulletin boards. Expect to pay upwards of $50–$100 an hour for their services.

Sign Up Early!

You can register for these prep courses as early as your first semester in law school or as late as your last, but there are two advantages to registering early: Both BAR/BRI and PMBR will freeze the cost of their courses as soon as you put down your deposit, so thinking ahead can save you several hundred dollars; early birds also benefit from supplementary prep materials—study outlines for your MPRE, for example—and subject guides for core law school classes to help you make the most of your law school experience.

So now that you know the ins and outs of this legal test of all tests, all you need to do is take the darn thing. Then, just sit back, relax (Ha!), and wait for four months to find out if you passed.

THE BIGGEST, BADDEST BAR

Want a close-up view of what it's like to take the bar? Jungle *followed one test-taker through the New York State exam.*

It's 6 A.M., three hours before the start of the July 24, 2001, New York State bar exam at Manhattan's Jacob K. Javits Convention Center, and the first arrivals are pacing.

Andrew Gershon, a Hofstra Law School alum, mills around a hallway above the still-locked exam rooms. He has decided he'd rather come here at this early hour than continue tossing and turning in his hotel room bed.

"You have the rest of your life going through your head," he says. "Sleep doesn't come easy." Jessica Greenberg, a University of Pennsylvania law grad, is Gershon's sole companion at the moment. She says she would have shown up even earlier had her father not suggested she attempt to get some more rest.

In the scheme of things, Gershon and Greenberg really aren't that early. In years past, jittery candidates have arrived at the Javits Center at 5 A.M. and waited outside for an hour before the security guards opened the doors. To soothe their nerves and kill some time, Gershon reads the *New York Post*. Greenberg listens to Kermit the Frog warble "The Rainbow Connection" through her headphones.

By 7:30, the corridor is thick with jumpy bar-takers. Just down the hall from Gershon and Greenberg, Mary Devin clutches a string of rosary beads blessed by the pope. Her boyfriend, John Hewitt, sits next to her. Despite the soupy July weather, Hewitt has outfitted himself in a frayed gray sweatshirt. "He wore that same Duke sweatshirt to every exam he took during law school," says Devin, who earned her JD from New York Law School. "He looks like a homeless person, but he thinks it retains knowledge. What can you do?"

Enter Amy Shuster. A 25-year-old New York University law grad, Shuster is confident she'll pass the bar, and she has reason to be. She was Phi Beta Kappa as an undergraduate at Johns Hopkins and an academic standout at NYU as well. But Shuster isn't just here to pass the test; it is her stated intention to remain cool, calm, and 100 percent collected in the process. "It's not healthy to be stressed, and it doesn't really help," she says.

A group of Shuster's former NYU classmates has gathered across the way. One woman looks like she might puke. A second appears ready to flat-out crack: "I cried four times yesterday! Four times!" she moans. Another pal of Shuster's is outwardly tranquil, but "he's taking medication that relaxes you—it slows your heart rate," Shuster says. "And he's wearing suntan lotion. He says the smell of the beach calms him."

To ensure that she didn't feel rushed, Shuster allowed almost two hours for the 20-minute cab ride from her apartment in Murray Hill. But now she's worried she may have arrived at the Javits Center a little too early. She does a few yoga stretches. "You'd never think a test," she says, "could cause so much anxiety."

The bar exam, no matter where it is given, is not a soothing experience. But no bar exam can match the nerve-fraying spectacle staged at the Javits Center each summer since 1988. Few states' tests are more demanding than New York's (California and Virginia are the only serious challengers). The Empire State's bar candidates, for starters, are expected to master roughly five times as much material as their neighbors in New Jersey. The 12-hour, 15-minute test is administered over two grueling days. On day one, which deals strictly with New York State law, candidates must write five essays, respond to 50 diabolically specific multiple-choice questions, and tackle the MPT, an exercise that asks them to incorporate a set of facts into a hypothetical memo or legal brief. Day two brings the MBE and with it another 200 maddening multiple-choice queries. And because New York is home to some of the world's best and brightest lawyers, virtually all of today's 5,525 test-takers will feel that the other 5,524 are somehow smarter and better prepared than they are.

Then there's the Javits Center. No other exam site in any state is as intimidating. The shining steel and smoked-glass complex, which occupies five city blocks along Eleventh Avenue on Manhattan's West Side, contains a cavernous 800,000 square feet of exhibition space. The brightly lit halls that serve as testing rooms stretch across more than five acres; they're typically used to stage conventions, but they'd be equally suited to housing jetliners.

Security is worthy of a presidential visit. An armored car, manned by armed guards, delivers the test packets early on the morning of day one. Nearly 300 proctors patrol the exam halls, and a 40-member security force guards both the entrances and the bathrooms, which are monitored to prevent candidates from sneaking crib sheets into the stalls. "We train our people on what to look for in potential cheaters," says logistics coordinator Armand Canestraro. "Have we been successful? Yes."

An ambulance is kept on standby, and though most medical emergencies have been routine (a pregnant woman going into labor, an elderly proctor having a high-blood-pressure attack), its presence doesn't exactly put one at ease. Mental health exigencies are another matter. Legend has it that a candidate once sprinted up and down the aisles sharing with her fellow test-takers this essential bit of information: "I am a covenant, and I am running with the land."

In spite of all this, roughly 70 percent of those who sit for the New York bar each July manage to pass. The overwhelming majority spring for expensive prep courses and log countless hours of private study. Most successful candidates have solid law school GPAs. But Bob Cohen, an associate director with BAR/BRI, the most popular bar review course, emphasizes that good grades don't guarantee exam success. "Some top students, because they are top students, think they know how to do the preparation," he says. "They disrespect the process, and they wind up flunking."

Those who fail the test must wait until February of the next year to try again. During the run-up to their second attempt, many will have to squeeze in their studying while also attempting to hold down or look for a job. Working lawyers have the added joy of sharing the news of their failure with their boss.

Shortly after 8:15, the candidates are allowed to enter their appointed exam rooms. As they funnel down the escalators that lead to Halls 1A, 1B, and 1C, the prevailing mood is one of woe: People waiting in line at the DMV look happier.

Once inside their respective halls, most candidates head directly to their assigned seats. Others beeline for the bathrooms, which, like the rest of the floor, had been off-limits while the proctors placed the test packets on the candidates' tables.

A voice, Oz-like, booms from a concert-strength sound system. It belongs to Bryan Williams, a nattily dressed member of the New York State Board of Law Examiners who is speaking from a small office across from the central hall, out of the test-takers' view. "Make sure that your seat number matches your test number," The Voice commands.

Despite the warning, a wayward would-be attorney in Hall 1A plops down one row behind where he belongs. The resulting chain reaction temporarily displaces two dozen of his cohorts, who are apparently too preoccupied to realize that they, too, are in the wrong seats. Had a proctor not intervened, disaster might have ensued. The tests are scored blindly (candidates are identified only by seat number), so sitting in the wrong spot can result in receiving someone else's score.

Shuster's seat is toward the front of Hall 1B. She is just settling into her chair when security guards lower the industrial-grade metal garage doors at 8:55. "I felt a big adrenaline rush," she says later. "I knew I was ready, and I wanted to just dive in."

Following what BAR/BRI describes as an "ideal" approach, Shuster began preparing for the test two months ago, just after Memorial Day. Her studying consisted of two phases. For the first six weeks, she spent from 9 A.M. to 1 P.M., Monday through Friday, in a BAR/BRI classroom. She then logged another six hours each day going over her notes on her own and answering practice questions. One day each weekend was reserved for downtime, at least until the BAR/BRI course ended. After that, attempting to master the test material became an eight-hours-a-day, seven-days-a-week job. "There's comfort in knowing that the same steps have worked for so many people," Shuster says.

In deciding what to study, Shuster also stuck to the BAR/BRI game plan. The vast majority of her effort was devoted to the material tested on the MBE: contracts, constitutional law, criminal law, evidence, property, and torts. Those topics would appear not only on the MBE but also on the New York portion of the test. Shuster spent weeks studying those subjects, and no more than 10 hours each on the 11 disciplines that could only come up, if they came up at all, during the New York–specific sections.

That's not to say Shuster toed the bar prep line completely. Rather than take her BAR/BRI course at the center closest to her apartment—the popular Times Square location, where a number of the 1,000 or so students lined up half an hour before class to scurry for front-row seats—she signed up for the relatively laid-back lessons at Manhattan's Fordham University Law School. Whenever possible, she left Manhattan and decamped to her boyfriend's parents' house in the Hamptons, which allowed her to punctuate her study sessions with sea kayaking and long strolls on the beach. And right before entering the stretch run, she gave herself . . . a vacation. "I didn't study on the Fourth of July," she says, "and all of my friends were like, 'I can't believe you took the day off!'"

Shuster's comparatively mellow approach can be traced back to her second year at NYU, when the former state high school debate champion from Guilford, Connecticut, resolved to become a sort of anti-McBeal. "I was so burnt out after the first year, I just didn't have the energy to be stressed anymore," she says. "I tried to make a transition to be more relaxed. After my first set of exams that semester, I found that I hadn't pushed myself so hard, yet I had done just as well, if not better."

At precisely 9 A.M., The Voice proclaims, "You may begin!" Shuster has decided that she will tackle the day-one essays in order, without looking ahead. "I worried that if I looked ahead, I might freak out," she says. The first of the three essays she'll need to face before lunch deals with a contract between two merchants, an issue she knows well. Nevertheless, it takes her a while to establish a rhythm, and her response eats up more time than the recommended 40 minutes. But she gets back on track during the next two essays—one on a felony murder, the other on domestic relations and professional responsibility. At 11 A.M.—right on schedule—she turns to the 50 multiple-choice questions that stand between her and the 12:15 break.

Many of the multiple-choice problems are dense riddles, and Shuster's answers sometimes rely as much on hunches as they do on facts. She knows some conjecture is okay: Because points are not subtracted for incorrect answers, it makes sense to hazard a guess on every question. Besides, she knows that candidates can get up to half of the 50 multiple-choice questions on the New York portion wrong and still pass the bar.

Shortly after 11, a Columbia Law School alum and soon-to-be Cravath, Swaine & Moore associate arrives at the entrance to the Javits Center. Having mismarked his calendar, he thought the test started on July 25 (tomorrow), not July 24 (today), and he realized his mistake just this morning. He asks a representative of the Board of Law Examiners if he may begin taking the test during the afternoon session, but the rules state that candidates must arrive at the test center no later than 9:30. Request denied. Casualty number one.

The lunch break is called at 12:15, and Shuster and the other test-takers stream out of the exam halls. Upstairs, the candidates organize themselves like high-schoolers at recess. There's a clique of smokers, a group of flash-card-wielding study freaks, and a few loners saying nothing and staring straight ahead. Shuster and a friend sit together and tuck into their lunches.

Though the Javits Center offers a few overpriced eateries, the majority of candidates bring their own sustenance. The Board of Law Examiners asks only that food be "quiet"; snacking is even permitted during the sessions, so long as one's victuals do not snap, crackle, or pop. While most candidates use the break to refuel, there are those, like Gershon, who do not ingest a morsel, lest digestion dull their mental edge.

Just down the hall from Shuster, one of the loners, a burly, dark-haired guy, keeps his nose buried in his study aids straight through to 1:30. Then, scrambling into Hall 1B, he almost gives the ambulance crew something to do by failing to notice that the metal door is about to close on his head.

At least he makes it back inside: A guy who had been sitting next to Mary Devin does not return at all. "In the morning session, I noticed he was sort of staring off into the distance," Devin reports. "I thought to myself, 'Maybe this isn't for him.'"

Opening her packet to start the afternoon session, Shuster flips to the 90-minute MPT. Twenty-six other jurisdictions use the MPT, but this is the first time it has appeared on the New York exam.

Designed to measure actual lawyering skills—as opposed to legal arcana—the MPT is an attempt to counter the long-standing criticism that the bar is not an accurate method of evaluating the worthiness of would-be attorneys. Since the MPT counts for only 10 percent of the final grade, some candidates feel they have little to gain by studying for it. But Shuster has made certain she's ready for it. "I see it as a good way to get points for minimal work," she says.

Turning to the first of the afternoon essays, Shuster sees that Lady Luck is smiling on her. New York practice, the topic she most dreads, did not figure in the morning essays, and this afternoon's first question is on torts. She handles it assuredly. Ditto for the next—and last—essay, which deals with wills.

Shuster completes the afternoon section a few minutes ahead of time. For a moment, she's tempted to reread her answers, but then she reconsiders: "I was, like, no, I'll just make myself upset if I see a mistake."

For the day, Shuster gives herself a 9 out of 10 for knowing her stuff and a 9 for staying calm. But as she walks home, another test-taker—a stranger—approaches. Having overheard Shuster's conversation with a reporter, the woman wants to know how Shuster handled a portion of the essay question that dealt with the evidentiary admissibility of a statement made by a dying man. "I can't believe someone would stop a random person and ask them about the bar," Shuster says. "What if I had said, 'Oh my God, that wasn't the answer— and if you didn't get that right, you failed!'"

On Wednesday morning, jaws inside the Javits Center are visibly less clenched than they had been 24 hours earlier, and the lighter mood is reflected in the candidates' sartorial choices. One man looks disco-ready in a faux snakeskin shirt. His female counterpart, a sort of Long Island version of Reese Witherspoon's character in *Legally Blonde*, wears a see-through blouse over a plunging T-shirt. "I see these girls in little tube tops, and I'm like, 'What?'" says Devin. Her boyfriend is wearing not only the same lucky sweatshirt as the day before but the same khakis as well.

Shuster, feeling more confident, heads off for the exam 30 minutes later than she did on Tuesday. "I've already taken two full practice MBEs," she says, referring to the dry runs she completed as part of her BAR/BRI course. "And I've done reasonably well."

With its 200 multiple-choice questions, the six-hour MBE leaves little time for dawdling, so the key to managing it successfully is to maintain a steady stride. Shuster believes she has a strong grasp on the MBE subject matter, but she also knows that she can run into trouble if she falls behind the BAR/BRI-approved schedule. Averaging 1.8 minutes per question, she should be on no. 17 at 9:30 A.M., no. 35 at 10 A.M., and so on, until time is called at noon.

Because there is so little room for error, Shuster has ruled out the possibility of a midsession bathroom break, as the round-trip could take up to five minutes. Others appear to be mindful of this potential complication as well. Rumor has it that one man is wearing a diaper.

As The Voice kicks off the morning session, the candidates quickly discover that fatigue has become a factor: In Hall 1A, a woman falls asleep while trying to answer a question. Shuster, meanwhile, has gotten herself into a groove, and she's exceeding the minimum pace, in part by not dwelling on questions that stump her. Once again, she finishes early. And once again, she resists the urge to double back and second-guess herself.

Compared with Tuesday's lunch hour, Wednesday's is downright festive. Socializers far outnumber studiers, and plans for postexam bacchanalia are the topic of more than one conversation. Shuster shuns talk of the test, but she does own up to the fact that the experience is wearing her down. "All those bubbles!" she says.

By 1:20 P.M., most candidates have returned to their seats, eager to get the ordeal over with. Once the afternoon session starts, however, many examinees begin to sputter. Shuster starts to flag as she reaches question no. 185. She has to read each query several times.

Late in the afternoon, someone knocks over a bottle, which shatters as it hits the concrete floor. Shuster, deep in a final run to the finish line, does not even look up.

At 4:30 P.M., 12 hours and 15 minutes into the test, The Voice declares an end to the proceedings. Shuster rises to her feet and makes eye contact with a stranger standing nearby. The two break into smiles.

The security guards slowly raise the garage door to Hall 1B, and a few candidates duck through the opening as soon as it reaches waist height. Having served their sentence, they are not willing to wait a moment longer for freedom.

Once the door is all the way open, the candidates pour out en masse. They are greeted by small groups of well-wishers—friends, family members, and significant others. Promoters handing out flyers for parties at Manhattan bars and restaurants are there, too (why the World Wrestling Federation thinks exhausted would-be lawyers might want to frequent its Times Square establishment is anyone's guess).

Many of the test-takers wear weary grins. Others can muster only yawns. At least one woman looks to be holding back tears. Devin is visibly upset as well. "I thought I'd be so happy coming out of that test," she says. "But Mother of God, that afternoon section was terrible."

Many candidates, in fact, feel like they were ambushed by unduly tricky questions during the last half of the MBE. Shuster agrees that parts of day two have been tough. But as far as she can tell, she has passed the test—and without getting too stressed. "I'm proud of myself," she says. "I stayed positive, and I just kept going."

When Shuster is about halfway home, the sky, gray all day, gives way to a summer downpour. "I'll feel more excited when I get the results," she says. (The news won't come for four months.) "You have to wait so long before you know how you did. You don't want to be too relieved, because for all you know, you could be taking the test again in February."

Then she adds, "You should put a big caveat in your story: Amy's big concern is having this article written about how confident she was, then she fails, and everyone makes fun of her.

"That," she says, "is one thing I'm stressed about."

Epilogue

Amy Shuster passed the bar. She accepted a job as an associate at Sullivan & Cromwell. Andrew Gershon and Jessica Greenberg also passed. John Hewitt passed, but his girlfriend, Mary Devin, did not. The guy who showed up late and was turned away? He signed up to take the next available test.

Note: Amy Shuster agreed to use her real name in this story. The other test-takers' names were changed.

Inspiration

· ·

- Erin Brockovich
- Justice John Paul Stevens
- Robert F. Kennedy Jr.
- Richard "Dickie" Scruggs
- Stephen Bright
- Vernon Jordan

AS YOU CONTEMPLATE A LEGAL CAREER, CONSIDER THE WISDOM OF THESE SIX LEGAL LUMINARIES, EACH INTERVIEWED BY *JD JUNGLE* BETWEEN 2001 AND 2002.

ERIN BROCKOVICH
Interviewed in September 2002

In 1993, Erin Brockovich and attorney Ed Masry filed a class-action lawsuit against the Pacific Gas and Electric Company for contaminating the groundwater in Hinkley, California. Brockovich, who began working for Masry as an office assistant, took it upon herself to research the matter, and through a combination of hard work, pluck, and crack investigative skills she assembled a mountain of evidence against PG&E. The claim: The company had poisoned the citizens of Hinkley by fouling their water with a toxic chemical called hexavalent chromium, or C-6. In 1996, PG&E settled the case and agreed to pay the plaintiffs $333 million. The story was made into the 2000 feature film *Erin Brockovich*, and Brockovich herself became a modern American folk hero. *JD Jungle* caught up with the toxic crusader to talk about what she's up to now. She spoke with trademark candor.

JD JUNGLE   You're suing PG&E again, this time for contaminating groundwater in Kettleman, California. Where does the case stand?

ERIN BROCKOVICH   We're going through motions. I uncovered this case in 1995, but this one's taken a lot longer than Hinkley because PG&E pulled that clever move, and filed for bankruptcy last year, which slowed us down. Right now, we're trying to pick a trial date. I hope it'll be soon. I'm guessing six months to a year.

JD   A lot of lawyers would kill to have your nose for a case. How do you do it?

EB   I'm not an expert. I'm not a rocket scientist. I'm not a lawyer. But I have compassion, and I have the ability to listen to people's suffering, to see that somebody is frightened, sick, dying. In Hinkley, I didn't see just one person, but two, three, four, five, six, seven, eight, nine, ten.

I would drive home and think, "Why would people unknown to each other make up lies about cows having tumors all over their body, or about dogs drinking water and then running around in circles and dropping dead, or about everybody having nosebleeds?" Do I have to be a rocket scientist to stop and think, "Gosh, maybe something's wrong?" That's where I begin my work. Then I ask questions, and I go into the local agencies, and I look through the files, and I look at the documents. From there, it's like putting the pieces of a puzzle together.

JD   How did you uncover the Kettleman case?

EB   While I was working on Hinkley, I'd gotten tips from
PG&E employees—things like, "You really need to look at
Kettleman." So Ed and I went out there, and we looked
around, and he said, "I don't think there's anything here,
kid. Let's go." But just as we were getting ready to leave, I
saw some tamarisk trees that looked like trees I'd seen in
Hinkley. They had this white substance on their leaves. I
had learned in Hinkley that a tamarisk will secrete a poison
through its leaves. The Hinkley case was in full gear at the
time, so Ed said, "I know what you're thinking, but I don't
want you coming back here." And I said, "Okay." The next
day, I got in my car and drove straight to the water board in
Fresno. One of the first documents I found was a letter
from the United States Department of the Interior, dating
back to the '60s, notifying PG&E in San Francisco that they
had excessive hexavalent chromium in one of their on-site
wells about 10 miles north of Kettleman. I thought, "Here
we go again."

JD   How much money are you seeking in this case?

EB   I think it should be about the same dollar value as Hinkley. It's just as bad. The number of people affected is roughly
the same, maybe a little bit more. They have the same illnesses and problems as the people in Hinkley—nosebleeds, a
lot of kidney problems, people with Crohn's disease, on
colostomy bags.

JD   Your critics say you're out to destroy corporate America.
What do you say to that?

EB   Big companies like to say that about me, but I like corporate America as much as anybody else. I like a nice car, and
I like nice things. But when I see corporations that have the
resources and the technology to protect human health and
human life—like the companies Ed and I have litigation

against—I think it's their duty to do that. Our job is to try and hold them accountable.

JD   What do you think about the Enron case and the other corporate scandals going on now?

EB   I can't believe the ego in corporate America. What, you think you're never going to get caught? Enron thought that. PG&E thought that. I remember a conversation with Ed back in 1992 about PG&E. I told him, "It will be their ego that will be their demise." If these corporations had more to lose than just money, maybe they wouldn't do it. If people on their boards had to face criminal charges, maybe they'd think twice.

JD   You live in California. Is PG&E your electric company?

EB   No, Southern California Edison is my provider. I've never had a problem with them. PG&E would probably cut me off.

JD   After the Hinkley case, Ed Masry gave you a $2.5 million bonus. You moved into an expensive new house that had to be gutted to get rid of toxic mold. Weird, huh?

EB   I wouldn't have believed this had I not been through it myself. I work on a toxic case. They make a movie about it. I get a bonus from it. Then I go and buy a toxic-mold home. I must carry around a neon sign that says toxic.

JD   You have two television shows in the works: one for NBC and one for Lifetime. Will you be the new Oprah?

EB   I can't talk about the specifics yet, but they will involve the same kind of work I've been doing—with people, with the environment, with illness. I wouldn't want to do a show for entertainment value, but for educational purposes. I like *48 Hours* and *20/20*. They teach me something. I like women like Barbara Walters and Diane Sawyer.

JD   When you look back at the movie, what's the one thing it got wrong about you?

EB   In general, it came across well. I'm passionate about my work, and they captured that passion. The only thing that wasn't really right is that very rarely will you see me with my bra straps hanging out. I wear low-cut tops, but my straps aren't showing. And you wouldn't see me wearing a leopard-print bra underneath a black sheer top, either. If I wore a sheer black top, I'd wear a sheer black bra. Leopard print doesn't look good underneath a black see-through shirt.

JD   Speaking of the way you dress, is it a good idea for a woman to display her sexuality at work?

EB   Yes. There are so many mixed messages for corporate lawyers, or any woman in the workplace. I mean, my gosh, we see what's out there in magazines. We know what's considered attractive. Yet when a woman in corporate America wants to show part of her sexuality, because it makes her feel good and that's a part of her, there's a backlash. That doesn't make sense to me. The way you dress should be no reflection of what you're capable of doing. Your clothes don't reflect what's in your brain or your heart. When I go to court, I'm respectful. I wear a blazer. But if I want to wear a bustier underneath it, you bet I will.

JD   Do you wish Julia Roberts stayed more committed to your work?

EB   No. I think she sent a message just by doing the movie. It's clear to me that she cares about America and she cares about people being poisoned. I wouldn't expect anything more from her.

JD What's the worst thing about fame?

EB One of the hardest things is the expectation that every case that comes to us is going to be another Hinkley. There are days when I come home feeling pretty bad because there's somebody who is truly suffering and we can't help them. Maybe we're not licensed to practice in their state. Or the facts aren't there. Sometimes there are statute problems. It's sad because there's hope that it will be another Hinkley, but it doesn't always turn out that way.

JD You're so visible now. Do you worry that people might start to tune you out? You know: "There's that woman hollering about toxic waste again."

EB I don't think about that. I am who I am. If something comes along where I think I can make a difference or maybe help somebody feel better about themselves, then I do it. I try to listen to my heart. That's what I follow.

JD You weren't so high on lawyers in the movie. What's your attitude toward them now?

EB There are lawyers who come forward and make a difference—people like Ed Masry. Lawyers like that believe in their client. They take the time to listen to their client. And they are some of the finest lawyers I know. But then for every lawyer I know like that, I meet ten who make me think, "My God. No wonder everyone hates lawyers!" Look at the defense attorneys I've seen. They demean you, they mock you, they make you feel stupid. And the turning of the words! They do it to every single client. "Isn't it true . . . ?" I hate that phrase. Everything starts with "Isn't it true?" For someone who isn't used to this, they have to stop and think, "Is it true? Is it not true?" The lawyers create that self-doubt. That's something that I cherish—that I can teach a client not to let that attorney make her doubt herself.

JD What's the best piece of advice you can give to lawyers?

EB One of the most important things for young lawyers to learn is ethics. Think of the people in charge at PG&E in the '60s—including their lawyers. I wonder what ethics class they missed. Had they made a different decision, they would have been responsible for saving hundreds of lives. When law students get out into the work world, their ethics are going to be challenged. And you know what, that new house, that new car, that raise, I'm telling you, I promise you, in the end, it will not be worth it if you got it covering up some dastardly deed.

JD Any other advice?

EB In every aspect of the law, somebody's coming to you because something is a big deal to them. They've been in a car wreck, they're getting divorced, they've been injured on a job, they drank poisoned water. In every case, there's a person on the other side who is passionate about what is happening to them. Lawyers are the ones who can make a difference for those people. Listen to them. It's not just about the book and the law that you're reading. It's about the person.

SUPREME COURT JUSTICE JOHN PAUL STEVENS
Interviewed in November 2001

John Paul Stevens is the Supreme Court's oldest sitting member. He is second in tenure only to Chief Justice William Rehnquist. And he is arguably the current Court's wisest member.

By "wisest," we do not mean that Stevens is necessarily the most intellectually gifted justice or that his opinions are necessarily the most just.

No, what we mean by "wisest" is that the man is *reasonable*. Whatever his judicial leanings (and he leans left), Stevens has earned a reputation on the high court as a smart and thorough thinker—a learned and honorable man who states his opinions with clarity and force but never shouts or bullies. He is a throwback to a less rancorous era, when law and politics were noble pursuits, not blood sports. The man is sensible. He is decent. He wears bow ties without irony. Call him the elder statesman of American justice.

Perhaps it's Stevens's midwestern heritage—and a lifetime of legal achievement—that account for his grounded judicial temperament. He was born in Chicago and received an AB in English literature from the University of Chicago in 1941. From 1942 to 1945, he served in the U.S. Navy, earning a Bronze Star. He graduated from Northwestern University School of Law in 1947 and received the highest grades given by the school up to that time. After clerking for Supreme Court justice Wiley Rutledge in 1947–1948, Stevens worked at two Chicago law firms from 1949 to 1970, then served on the U.S. Court of Appeals for the Seventh Circuit, in Chicago, from 1970 to 1975. He was appointed to the Supreme Court in 1975 by President Gerald Ford.

Now, as he begins his twenty-eighth year on the high court, Justice Stevens appears to be nearing retirement. The average age of the last five justices to leave the bench is 81, and rumors of departure have been circulating around Stevens (as well as Justices Rehnquist and Sandra Day O'Connor) for several years.

JD Jungle contributing editor Susan Estrich, who clerked for Stevens in 1977–1978, spoke to the justice about everything from his law career to your law career to the Court and the law today.

His reflections are, of course, wise.

SUSAN ESTRICH   What's your first memory of law school?

JOHN PAUL STEVENS   I was intimidated. The dean at Northwestern was Leon Green, an old-fashioned teacher who made everyone in the class stand up when he or she recited. He made a point of making young law students learn that being in court is a tough job, and you should learn to get pushed around by whoever's in charge.

ESTRICH   Did you get pushed around?

STEVENS   I did, and everybody else did, too. Most of my classmates had been officers in the war—they weren't timid souls. But he inspired fear in all of us.

ESTRICH   What's your best memory of law school?

STEVENS   I remember several inspiring teachers—Green . . . Nat Nathanson. Nathanson taught constitutional law and ad law, and I still think about him in my work. I had a wonderful class, too. I'm still convinced it's the best class that ever went through the school. I also remember playing bridge during the noon hour, but Dean Green, when he found out about that, he put an end to it.

ESTRICH   Did you have legal heroes in law school?

STEVENS   I'd say Justices [Benjamin] Cardozo, [Louis] Brandeis, and [Oliver Wendell] Holmes were heroes—and later Wiley Rutledge. They were generally the heroes of the profession, and I admired the opinions they had written. I gave a speech just last night in which I quoted a favorite remark by Justice Cardozo: "The work of a judge would be impossible if he couldn't lay his course on the basis of the bricks that had been laid by the men who had gone before."

ESTRICH   Were you good at law school?

STEVENS   To be honest, I was. My grades were all As.

ESTRICH   Do you remember how you felt after you took the bar exam?

STEVENS   Actually, I thought it was easy. The only thing I worried about was that I finished early, and I started wondering why everybody else was still taking the exam. I began to think maybe I'd blown it. I probably should have been more concerned about flunking. Now and then, some very good students do. You never know.

ESTRICH   What was the first case you worked on after law school?

STEVENS   I was an assistant to Ed Johnston, the senior partner of the firm I went with [Poppenhusen, Johnston, Thompson, and Raymond]. It was an antitrust case.

ESTRICH   What did you do?

STEVENS   I carried the books and did the legal research. I didn't have a case of my own for some time.

ESTRICH   Is there one case you've worked on over the years that you're especially proud of?

STEVENS   Yes, *Groppi* v. *Leslie*. It was decided when I was on the Court of Appeals. It was about a priest who had demonstrated on the floor of the Wisconsin legislature against some of the state's treatment of the underprivileged. He was held in contempt without a trial, and the court sustained the contempt finding. I wrote a dissent on the Court of Appeals in the en banc hearing, and the case was ultimately reversed in the Supreme Court. It was important to me for reasons that I won't try to cover in a brief interview. But its importance relates to the independence of the judiciary and calling them like you see them.

ESTRICH   What's your favorite book about the law?

STEVENS   If I had to pick one in a hurry, I'd pick Cardozo's *The Nature of the Judicial Process*. That's one I often look at.

ESTRICH   In law school, did you ever think about becoming a Supreme Court justice?

STEVENS   No.

ESTRICH   When did the thought occur?

STEVENS   When President Ford called me on the phone.

ESTRICH   Not even when you were on the circuit court?

STEVENS   I guess every judge thinks about that as a possibility, but I can't say I thought about it as a realistic possibility. I figured the odds were kind of long.

ESTRICH   How did you find out that you'd been nominated to the Supreme Court?

STEVENS   I was nominated on the day after Thanksgiving in 1975. I knew that I was under consideration a few days earlier. Shortly after Justice [William] Douglas resigned, Bob Sprecher, a fellow judge on the Court of Appeals, called me and said that the American Bar Association had contacted him to ask him about me because they had been asked to do background checks on people under consideration. There were stories in the newspapers that gave the so-called preferred list. But I didn't know that I was actually going to be the president's choice until that day after Thanksgiving. I was in the office and the phone rang and somebody said, "The White House is calling." Then President Ford told me he had decided to appoint me.

ESTRICH   What went through your head?

STEVENS   I was delighted, of course, and humbled. It's a very moving experience.

ESTRICH   Did you celebrate?

STEVENS   It's a strange story. My good friend Phil Tone, who was also on the Court of Appeals, was also one of those considered. Between the time the vacancy occurred and the actual appointment, we met and agreed that if either of us heard from the White House, he would immediately tell the other. So the president called that day, late in the morning, and he asked me not to tell anyone the news because they wanted to announce it from Washington and not have it leaked. I said, "Well, Mr. President, I have this understanding with Judge Tone." I explained, and the president said, "I think he'll understand if you just tell him I asked you not to say anything about it." I honored his request—I guess I did tell my mother—and later that day, the phone rang, and it was the White House again. This time, it wasn't President Ford but someone else. He said, "The president told us about your agreement with Judge Tone. You can go tell Judge Tone now because we're going to announce it in about half an hour." It seemed to me quite an insight into the kind of person the president is that he would understand why that was important to me. Phil Tone walked into the office at that moment—the rumor was already all over the building—and congratulated me.

ESTRICH   You're the oldest justice on a Court that's delicately balanced between conservatives and liberals. Do you feel pressure not to retire in order to maintain that balance?

STEVENS   No, I don't. Retirement is something I'll have to decide on when I think I'm no longer able to function as effectively as I should. There's a balance, because on the one hand, you have a special asset in having the experience on the Court that some of the others don't have. On the other hand, you always have to guard against the danger that you're relying more on law clerks than you should be and not doing your own work.

ESTRICH   On this Court, you're frequently in the minority. Is that frustrating?

STEVENS   That's something one never is happy about—it's been true since I was on the Court of Appeals. When you're in dissent, you know one of two things: Either the Court's wrong or you're wrong, and you don't want either of those things to be true. So you'd rather not be in dissent. There's no doubt about that.

ESTRICH   There's been a great deal of speculation in the wake of *Bush* v. *Gore* that this Court is now bitterly divided. Do you and your colleagues get along?

STEVENS   Yes, we get along.

ESTRICH   Can you give an example?

STEVENS   Well, if you ask any member of the Court about personal relationships, you'll find that everybody will give you the same answer, and everyone is speaking truthfully.

ESTRICH   Because of *Bush* v. *Gore*, many people think of this Court as inherently political. Your own dissent took on the Court quite eloquently. In light of that, how do you maintain respect for the Court as an institution?

STEVENS   There are aspects of that question that could take a long time to answer. I think the way all of us try to maintain respect for the Court is by continuing to do our work as best we can.

ESTRICH   Do you think that decision has had a bad effect on the public or on the Court?

STEVENS   That's one case I'd just as soon not talk more about.

ESTRICH   The process of nominating justices to the Court has become bitterly political. Is that bad for America?

STEVENS   I'd rather not summarize my views off the top of my head, but I think it's become more political than it should be.

ESTRICH   Since you started your career, what's the biggest change in the way law is practiced?

STEVENS   When I was first hired, it was by a firm that hired four lawyers at the time and jumped from 24 to 28, and that was a major law firm. Now that's called a boutique. Today you have these huge law firms, and I don't understand how they can be managed effectively and have everyone act as professionally as they have to.

ESTRICH   Do you think the emphasis on salaries has changed the law for the worse?

STEVENS   I don't know, but it does seem strange that a young lawyer a year out of law school, or a year after clerking, immediately makes more money than the judge for whom he or she was working.

ESTRICH   If you were graduating from law school today, would you go to a large firm? Or would you strike out on your own?

STEVENS   I think I might well go to a firm for a few years. That's what I did. I spent four years with [Poppenhusen, Johnston, Thompson, and Raymond], then two of the other lawyers and I left and formed our own firm [Rothschild, Stevens, Barry, and Myers]. I think it's important to get practical experience.

ESTRICH   A lot of law students struggle with whether they should take a high-paying corporate law job or follow their ideals into something lower-paying but more personally rewarding. What's your advice?

STEVENS   Well, my advice comes from a period when the average law school graduate didn't have staggering loans to pay off. That said, I'd repeat the advice that Willard Pedrick, an instructor at Northwestern, gave to me and others: Do what you want to do next and don't think too far ahead. If you find something that's challenging and interesting, do it now, and make the pecuniary reward a secondary consideration. I don't think students should foreclose private practice—you can get a lot of interesting assignments. I don't think you should foreclose on making money. But don't let it be the dominant consideration.

ESTRICH   What do you look for in a law clerk?

STEVENS   Someone like you.

ESTRICH   I love that. Now, what's the real answer?

STEVENS   All clerks are different; there's no standard mold. That's one of the joys of the job—interviewing and hiring clerks. You meet wonderful people.

ESTRICH   What's the most important piece of advice you would give to young lawyers?

STEVENS   Work hard, and remember the importance of making sure people know your word is good. The most important asset a lawyer has is having other people being willing to trust him or her in his representations of both the facts and the law. I think young lawyers—many lawyers, now and then—fail to appreciate how important it is to be totally honest with your clients and with your adversaries and with the court.

ESTRICH   What's the most important piece of advice you would give to anxious new law students who may be wondering if they're going to make it in this profession?

STEVENS   The coursework is by far the most important. Work hard. Do your best, and don't give up.

ROBERT F. KENNEDY JR.
Interviewed in September 2001

Except for his name, Robert F. Kennedy Jr. started out in the law like a lot of people. As a young man, he decided to go to law school, and after earning his JD from the University of Virginia in 1982, he became a prosecutor. All well and good. But then he decided to veer off into a budding form of environmental law. He began suing on behalf of . . . a river. Specifically, the Hudson River. He helped popularize the strategy of appointing a guardian, or "Riverkeeper," for a given body of water—a practice now used from the Hudson to the San Francisco Bay—then suing those who foul the waters.

Today, the 48-year-old Kennedy is the chief prosecuting attorney for the Hudson Riverkeeper, codirector of the Pace University Environmental Litigation Clinic, and senior attorney for the Natural Resources Defense Council. With George W. Bush viewed by environmentalists as aggressively antigreen, Kennedy argues that now is a critical time for young attorneys to enter environmental law. His call to action and his passion for his own work have brought new energy to an old Kennedy ideal: the value of putting social service before self-interest.

JD JUNGLE   Grade the Bush record on the environment.

ROBERT F. KENNEDY JR.   It's worse than that of any president in a century. His visit to the Everglades [during the summer of 2000] is a perfect example. He announced more than
$200 million in aid, but that number represents a substantial
cut from what the Everglades was supposed to get under the
Clinton plan. Because we have a very docile press, they cover
these things as if they were something good. But Bush's an-
nouncement was a cut. It was an attack on the Everglades. In
Texas, Bush had the worst environmental record of any governor in the country. Under his leadership, Texas had some of
the highest levels of air pollution, toxic releases, and water
pollution in the 50 states. His environmental commissioners
came from the regulated industries. One of the heads of the
Texas Natural Resource Conservation Commission (the state
environmental protection agency) was a 30-year executive of
the Monsanto [chemical] Company. And Bush has brought
the same philosophy to Capitol Hill. Look at his appointment
of Christie Todd Whitman to the Environmental Protection
Agency. As governor of New Jersey, she cut the budget for the
state's Department of Environmental Protection by almost a
third. The person she brought in to run DEP was a political
hack from south Jersey. He essentially ended environmental
enforcement in the state, and Whitman's motto was "New
Jersey is open for business."

JD   Has George W. Bush done anything at all that's good
for the environment?

RFK   I wish there were something good to say, but there
isn't. Gale Norton, his secretary of the interior, is a joke. She
has argued in front of the Supreme Court that the Endangered Species Act and the Surface Mining Act are unconsti-
tutional. She doesn't appear to believe in public lands. She
seems to think they should all be privatized. Now she's the

principal enforcer of the Endangered Species Act and the Surface Mining Act and the principal trustee of more than 400 million acres of our nation's public lands. Spencer Abraham, who is in charge of the Department of Energy, coauthored a bill when he was in Congress to dismantle the same department. And the lower-level officials being brought into the Cabinet departments are conservative ideologues in line with the Heritage Foundation and the Federalist Society, while the scientists are being pushed aside. The agencies are being systematically turned over to large corporations whose executives see antipollution laws as interfering with their profit-taking. Listen, the EPA's budget was more than $7 billion under the Clinton administration—0.4 percent of the federal budget. Bush has proposed to cut that by half a billion, and he's got at least another quarter of a billion in cuts in mind for the Interior Department.

JD One of Al Gore's weaknesses as a presidential candidate was the perception that he was too green. How should a presidential nominee in 2004 describe his environmental platform?

RFK I disagree. Gore's primary problem was that he was seen as someone who was not passionate about anything. If he'd spoken out more about the environment, he would have done a lot better. Polling I've seen has shown that Americans, both Republicans and Democrats, were worried about Bush's environmental record in Texas, and I think if Gore had done a better job of getting that out before the public, he would have won the election. The environment is intertwined with every other important social issue. It's the most important social issue.

JD How so?

RFK Poverty and race issues are inseparable from environmental issues. Look at where the toxic dumps go in this country. They always go into a black or Hispanic neighborhood.

Blacks and Hispanics are far more likely to live in an environ-
mentally contaminated community than whites. One of the
largest toxic-waste dumps in the country is in Emelle, Al-
abama, 93 percent black. One of the largest concentrations of
toxic-waste dumps is in the South Side of Chicago. One of the
most contaminated ZIP codes in California is East L.A.'s. The
poor always bear the heaviest burden for environmental injury, whether it's access to public lands or exposure to toxic
chemicals, so this is a fundamental issue. It's not just about
protecting fish and birds for their own sake.

JD   Grade Bill Clinton's environmental record.

RFK   His was a rearguard action that he fought against the
Gingrich Congresses—the 104th and 105th—which were two
of the most anti-environmental Congresses in American history. They tried to dismantle 30 years of environmental action. Clinton stood up to them, and ultimately they shut
down the government. The government shutdown was because of environmental riders that the Republicans had at-
tached to the Omnibus Budget Bill. Clinton said no to them,
and they shut down the government. He stood up for us.

JD   Say I'm a second-year law student. My best friend is at
Skadden, Arps, making the big bucks while I'm working at a
low-paying environmental law job. He says to me, "You're
a sucker." How do I answer him?

RFK   People have felt that way for ages. But there is a
choice in life. You can make a big pile of money for yourself,
or you can spend your life being of service to others. My own
experience and my observation of others have taught me that
being of service is a more worthwhile way to spend your life.
If what you seek is peace of mind and happiness, then that's
the path. People have different philosophies, and I don't be-
grudge them that. I make choices in order to look at myself in
the mirror and have some peace of mind.

JD   If I were a law student interested in getting into environmental law, what's the most effective kind of work I could do next summer?

RFK   You could come and work for us at the Pace University Environmental Litigation Clinic in White Plains, New York. We give each student four polluters to sue, then they have the summer to litigate against polluters on the Hudson or some other waterway. We also have volunteer jobs every summer.

JD   Where did the Riverkeeper idea come from?

RFK   The first Riverkeeper was founded on the Hudson in 1966 by a blue-collar coalition of commercial and recreational fishermen. Most were veterans of World War II and Korea who had worked on the Hudson as commercial fishermen. Their livelihoods were being destroyed by large polluters, mainly Penn Central Railroad, which was vomiting oil from a four-and-a-half-foot pipe. The shad tasted of diesel, so it couldn't be sold at the Fulton Fish Market, in New York City. All these people, about 300 of them, got together in an American Legion hall, and someone suggested that they light a match to the oil slick to blow up the pipe. Someone else said that they should jam a mattress up the pipe and flood the rail yard with its own waste. Somebody else suggested they float a raft of dynamite into the intake of the Indian Point power plant, which at that time was killing a million fish a day on its intake screen, taking food off their families' tables.

Then a former Marine named Bob Boyle stood up. He was a writer for *Sports Illustrated*. He was a great fly fisherman, and two years before, he had written an article about angling on the Hudson. In researching the story, he'd come across an ancient navigational statute called the 1888 Rivers and Harbors Act, which made it illegal to pollute any waterway in the United States. There was also a bounty provision that said that anyone who turned in the polluter got to keep half of the fine. Boyle persuaded these people that instead of breaking the law, they should be enforcing it. The bounty provision had never been enforced—not a single time. These guys were the first ones to do it. They shut down the Penn Central pipeline 18 months later. They got $2,000, and they used that money to finance investigations into Ciba-Geigy, Anaconda Wire & Cable, and Exxon—some of the biggest corporations in America. They got a $200,000 bounty in one case, and they spent the money on a boat. In 1983, they hired a full-time riverkeeper—John Cronin, a former commercial fisherman. Later they hired me as the prosecutor, again using bounty money. Altogether, we've now fought more than 100 success-ful lawsuits against Hudson River polluters.

JD   You're a Kennedy; you could have practiced any kind of law in the world. What attracted you to the environment?

RFK   I didn't study it when I was in law school, but I was al-ways interested in the environment. I became a prosecutor af-terward, and around 1984 I decided I wanted to do something that was consistent with my values. I have spent a lot of time on the Hudson, catching fish and now investigating polluters and getting to know the river and the fishermen who are my clients. I love it. I love what I do.

JD   What makes the environment so important to you?

RFK   The environment is the best measure of how our democracy is working. It's how we distribute the goods of the land. In the past, whenever we hit a depression in New York State and people were unemployed, they could always go down to the river and fish. It was the social safety net. You could always find fish in the river, and they belonged to the people. But now they are too dangerous to eat. The barge traffic on the upper river has been shut down because the shipping channels are too toxic. Women all along the upper Hudson are likely to have elevated levels of PCBs in their breast milk. Acres of beautiful shorefront property are off the tax rolls, robbed from the communities as a source of revenue or recreation. Virtually all of the commercial fishermen on the Hudson are out of work because, although the Hudson is loaded with fish, almost all of the fish are still loaded with General Electric's PCBs and are too toxic to sell. Countless people living in the Hudson Valley have General Electric's PCBs in their flesh and in their organs. That's a theft. That's an active theft. The fish and the waterways are owned by the people. Everybody has a right to use them. Nobody has a right to use them in a way that will diminish their use or en-joyment by others. It's a kind of right that dates back to the Magna Carta. And General Electric has come in and stolen the fish from everybody in the state. We don't own them now. We can't use them. General Electric liquidated them for cash. They turned them into profit, and they left behind a giant mess. That's a profound injustice.

JD   Is cleaning up a river a moral fight or an economic fight?

RFK   Good environmental policy is always, 100 percent of the time, good economic policy. If we want to measure our economy, then it should be based on how it produces jobs and the dignity of those jobs over the generations. What the Bush administration is urging us to do is to treat the planet like a business in liquidation—to have a few years of pollution-based prosperity. But our children will pay for our joyride with denuded landscapes, poor health, and cleanup costs they won't be able to afford. Environmental injury is a form of deficit spending.

JD   How does one articulate the Kennedy tradition of public service to a generation that seems pleased with itself and with the prosperity that comes from pursuing self-interest?

RFK Our nation's history is really a battle between two visions of this country. One of those visions is that America is a city on a hill, a model to the rest of the world for what human beings can accomplish if they work together and maintain their focus on a spiritual mission—trying to build communities. That idea really distinguished the European settlement of North America from the European conquest of Latin America, where the Europeans came as conquistadors driven by greed—to extract the minerals, to level the landscape, to subjugate the people, to enrich themselves, and then to move on. That very notion became prevalent in our country during the gold rush of 1849. That philosophy became the driving force behind the idea of Manifest Destiny and the driving force behind the robber barons of the 1880s and 1890s. Those two warring philosophies have provided the tension behind every major conflict in American history, from the Civil War to recent congressional elections. It can be felt in our own communities, at the planning board meetings when we have to decide whether to sell out to Wal-Mart for the easy money or to build a community that has dignity and maintain what our parents gave to us. And we have to fight that battle in our personal lives, as well. We each have to wake up in the morning and ask ourselves: Is this all about making my pile bigger? Am I going to be a gold digger? Or am I going to be somebody who has taken what God has given me and return it to my community? Is today going to be about me? Or is it going to be about giving back?

JD Will you ever run for political office?

RFK I considered running in the last Senate campaign in New York.

JD And in the future?

RFK We'll see.

RICHARD "DICKIE" SCRUGGS
Interviewed in February 2002

At the Sav-Rex drugstore and soda fountain in Pascagoula, Mississippi, a half-dozen regulars at the horseshoe-shaped lunch counter hand down a unanimous verdict on their neighbor Richard Scruggs. The native son turned trial lawyer legend, whose David-versus-Goliath triumph over Big Tobacco was immortalized in Michael Mann's *The Insider*, earns a decided thumbs-up from the foreman of this impromptu jury: "Dickie Scruggs is a down-to-earth, good person; he's done a lot for people—and done a lot for himself."

Dubbed by *Newsweek* "the most influential man in America that you've never heard of," Scruggs rose to prominence in Pascagoula in the early 1980s, shortly after hanging out his own shingle. In a company town dominated by Ingalls Shipbuilding, Scruggs sued the local industrial behemoth and won. Later, he earned a fortune representing thousands of Ingalls employees in personal injury claims against asbestos manufacturers.

But Scruggs stepped onto the national stage by taking on the world's biggest tobacco companies. Supported by the attorneys general of several states, he led a team of lawyers in a four-year war against Liggett Group, R.J. Reynolds Tobacco, Brown & Williamson, and other cigarette makers. Scruggs sought reimbursement for the cost of treating smoking-related illnesses under Medicaid. In 1997, he won a host of concessions from the tobacco companies—and a tidy little settlement of $240 billion.

Scruggs's modus operandi: Take on gargantuan opponents, then stick your neck out—way out—to win. When Mississippi attorney general Michael Moore recruited Scruggs to battle the tobacco companies, the state could not devote taxpayer dollars to litigation, so Scruggs bankrolled the case with millions of his own money. And when the state's key witness in that matter—former Brown & Williamson research director Jeffrey Wigand—faced a smear campaign, death threats, and a court order prohibiting his testimony, Scruggs opened his home to Wigand to protect him.

Recently, Scruggs opened his home to *JD Jungle*. In a wide-ranging interview held in "Al Pacino's dressing room" (aka the parlor of Scruggs's columned 1940s colonial overlooking the Gulf Coast), Scruggs recalled the peaks and valleys of the tobacco case, reflected on his other career highlights, and outlined the battle plan against his next adversary: the HMO industry.

JD JUNGLE   The tobacco companies once appeared invulnerable to lawsuits. What made you decide to take on such long odds?

DICKIE SCRUGGS   The same sort of motivation that Sir Edmund Hillary had when he climbed Mount Everest. It was the pinnacle—the legal equivalent of Mount Everest. Nobody had ever beaten these guys. We thought we could. We had the ideas and the legal theories. We had the skills and the legal resources. We had an attorney general, Mike Moore, who was willing to gamble his reputation on the whole thing. Maybe we were just young and dumb. Actually, we were very fortunate.

JD   Luck played a part?

DS   It was more than luck. We had providence. One of those things destiny commanded, and I don't know why. Not because we were the chosen few, but because, I think, the time had come. The political forces were right, and it turned out we had institutional allies we didn't know we had when we started.

JD   Such as . . .

DS   The national press corps was one, because the tobacco industry had just successfully sued ABC and had threatened to sue CBS. The press knew tobacco companies were a true threat to the First Amendment, so I don't think the industry got any breaks.

JD   Still, some people thought it was nuts to take on big tobacco.

DS   Let's put it this way: It was not prudent to take on the tobacco industry. Your entire fortune, your career, and everything else was on the line. But it basically took on the overtone of a crusade. I think when you're taking on something like that, you have to be totally dedicated beyond rationality. I won't say fanatical, because you have to use judgment in what you do, at least in your tactics. But there were many, many lawyers—good lawyers—who declined to be involved with us because they didn't think the suit could be won. They didn't think that the legal theories would support it or that the public would support it. And I think that in order to succeed, we had to—with an objective mind—become reckless.

JD   Did you ever pray during the battle?

DS   Oh, many times! I still do. Just to give thanks for getting through it. We had some near-death experiences during that thing. Not in a physical sense, but there were many times I thought that we were going to go down in flames.

JD   What was the toughest problem you faced?

DS   Probably the Jeffrey Wigand smear campaign. We had become so closely identified with Wigand [played by Russell Crowe in *The Insider*] that his credibility and our credibility had become linked; if he'd been discredited significantly, it would have set us way back.

JD   How much have you personally earned from the settlement?

DS   Oh, boy. That's hard to say. It depends on how you calculate it.

JD   Roughly.

DS   If you added it all up, hundreds of millions of dollars.

JD   Three hundred?

DS   Yeah, probably, but not a whole lot more than that. I haven't got that in the bank, if that's what you mean. That's paid out over 26 years.

JD   You've said that "lawyers who have made these sorts of fees have an obligation to invest them and create a resource for fighting against other wrongs in future litigation." Would you support a law mandating lawyers to pay a portion of their fees to a fund that supports public-interest law?

DS   I'm not sure I'd be willing to go that far. I sure would support a law that would make it easier for lawyers to do that. For example, by creating tax incentives or something like that.

JD   Rebut the *Providence Journal's* argument that "there is a word for the practice of targeting vulnerable businesses, and then by way of timely contributions, inducing the state to bring profitable lawsuits. And the word is *extortion*."

DS   I would agree with that statement, but I don't think it fits any situation that I've ever been involved in. What attorney general would risk his career taking on the tobacco industry for some lawyer who had contributed to his campaign?

Mike Moore would never do that. Mike Moore and I have been friends since the first day of law school. We're from the same hometown. That's why Mississippi took on the case, because he trusted me and I trusted him and we felt like we could do this, along with the other lawyers in our courtroom. I don't know of a single case where a lawyer made a timely contribution to an attorney general and got hired to sue a vulnerable industry. I mean, the tobacco industry was not vulnerable at that time.

JD   How do you assess whether to take on an industry?

DS   My criteria for taking a case is that the conduct being challenged has got to have a widespread effect on public health. Cigarettes and HMOs are sort of on different sides of that coin: tobacco makes people sick and puts them in the hospital; HMOs make people sick and keep them out of the hospital. Second, there has to be some threshold of outrage toward the industry's conduct. If somebody sells a product that turns out to hurt a lot of people, which satisfies the first criteria, but they just do it negligently—just screw up—then that doesn't satisfy my criteria. And the third criteria is that it has to be something that the courts are capable of fixing. There are a lot of social problems—gun control, for instance—that are not adjudicative. To me, the problem with guns is what do you do with 250 million guns that are already out there in people's hands? No court order is going to get rid of those guns.

JD   Outline your basic argument in the HMO case. Why are you right, and why is the other side wrong?

DS   Basically, we're saying that what the HMOs are guilty of is garden-variety consumer fraud. That you can gussy it up any way you want to, but they're selling something and not delivering. They promise you a parachute, if you will, of health care benefits such that if you need them, the parachute will open and give you a soft landing. But what happens if you need them is you pull the rip cord and you either get a streamer or a much smaller canopy and a lot harder landing than you bargained for.

JD David Boies is in on the HMO case. You and he seem to be an odd couple. Do you get along? Is his fame an asset or a liability for your case?

DS David is bright. He's a gentleman. He's got a good sense of when to speak up and when not to speak up. He's extremely articulate and has the ability to reduce what seem to be complex legal and factual issues down to their essence and explain them in common language. He's a very fine lawyer. I think that he's an asset for all those reasons. His fame speaks for itself and is well deserved.

JD Why were you in two rival camps initially?

DS Well, we didn't know what his camp was doing, and they didn't know what our camp was doing. To go after the HMOs, I put together a team of lawyers I had worked with in the tobacco case and in earlier asbestos litigation. David got together another group of lawyers and went after HMOs on a parallel track. And when the cases were consolidated and sent to one court, we essentially didn't have any choice but to work together. There were some fits and starts and some rough edges, but not between David and me—more between people from rival law firms in our respective organizations.

JD On a scale of 1 to 10, with 1 being a sure loss and 10 being a sure win, can you rate your chances against the HMOs?

DS I'd say an 8.

JD Critics say the HMO case, if successful, could lead to higher insurance costs, meaning more uninsured Americans. Is that a worthwhile gamble?

DS Yes. The choice is, do you want to pay a dollar and get 25 to 30 cents of coverage, or do you want to pay a dollar and a quarter and get a dollar and a quarter's worth of coverage? That's the difference. It may cost more, but you'll get what you pay for.

JD The producers of *The Insider* cast Michael Moore to play himself but cast an actor to portray you. Does it bother you that you're not more famous?

DS No, not at all. If I am going to be that influential, I'd rather be less known. I get more done that way. Mike's just a lot more telegenic than I am. I went to dinner with [producer-director] Michael Mann and Al Pacino. It was in the middle of the legislative battle over tobacco in 1998, and Mann asked me to read some lines. For about half an hour or so we read from the script, then went out and had dinner. Mike Moore joined us. And he had not even read, he just joined us at dinner. After I'd bought the dinner, Mike Mann leans over and says, "You know, Dick, you did a great job of reading that script. I'm probably going to get a professional actor to play your part." So I said, "Well, thanks a lot. After I pick up the check, you fire me."

JD What's your review of the movie?

DS If you had to condense four years or more into a two-and-a-half-hour film, it did a great job. There was nothing in it that was wrong or untrue. I think that the orchestration of the deposition was a little overblown in the sense that it really wasn't orchestrated by [former *60 Minutes* producer] Lowell

[Bergman]. Although he was there, it wasn't like he sat back and masterminded it, like in the movie. But he deserves an awful lot of credit for being there.

JD You went up against a host of white-shoe firms during the tobacco case. Did you ever detect arrogance?

DS I did. I never encountered anybody who was outright rude, but I felt there was a contempt that those lawyers had for me and for all of us in tobacco litigation. They considered us to be small-time lawyers, unworthy adversaries who they would be able to dispatch with ease. They miscalculated.

JD Do you have legal heroes?

DS Morris Dees and Gerry Spence. I've never met Morris Dees, but the guy has got tenacity and skill, and he has been able to challenge what seemed to be overwhelming forces and use his wits to succeed. The same with Gerry Spence. I mean, Spence is just a natural lawyer. He sounds crazy when you see him on TV, but he's very shrewd, and he has a great sense of what his audience wants to hear. I mean—my God—he walked Imelda Marcos.

JD Are you a natural?

DS In some things. I think my talent is putting together coalitions of lawyers and keeping them working together toward the same goal—coming up with a sensible strategy on how to get there. That's what I do. I mean, I'm okay in the courtroom, but there are a lot of lawyers who make better arguments than I do. Boies, for example. My skill is more like that of a successful head coach than a successful quarterback.

JD What's your biggest weakness as a lawyer?

DS Gullibility. Sometimes I trust people's motives too much. I think I'm easy to fool once.

JD Tobacco is obviously a big win. What was your biggest loss?

DS It was early in my career, when I was in my second year out of law school. I was sent up to a rural, largely African-American county in western Mississippi to defend—I was a defense lawyer when I first started practice—an electric power association against a claim by an itinerate black woman that the power company had somehow sent too much electricity to her house and set fire to it. Now, nobody was hurt, so she was suing for the value of the house. I didn't think I could lose, and I went up to try the case. Not only did I lose, but I had punitive damages returned against the company. It was an all-black jury, and all my witnesses were white men. They didn't do a very good job as witnesses, and I didn't do a very good job getting them prepared. We lost the case, and it was humiliating. The lawyer who beat me was a lawyer named Don Barrett—he and I became friends after he beat me. Don's family for several generations have been the dominant family in that rural county. The case was not won in the courtroom, it was won on the back roads. Don's family owned the bank; they own the whole county. And the jurors were not going to come back with a judgment against one of theirs. I was naïve enough to believe what happened in the courtroom was what mattered.

JD You were a fighter pilot during the height of the Cold War. What did you learn about the law from that experience?

DS Flying off an aircraft carrier for two and a half years is about as stressful as it gets in this life, and I think that helped me deal with the stress of law school and later big-time litigation. I also developed a bit of a knack for trying to figure out a way to penetrate an impenetrable object, so to speak. I was in charge of developing a set of tactics that would enable carrier airplanes, fighters and bombers, to penetrate Russian radar and missile screens of ships and to successfully attack them before they could launch their cruise missiles. That's what success as a lawyer really is. It's problem-solving.

JD Tell me about your first law firm job. You left in 1978 after just two years there.

DS I was a little older than most of the lawyers fresh out of law school. I'd been in the navy for five years before I went to law school, and I went to a firm in Jackson, Mississippi, that had a crusty old senior partner. He didn't like me, and I didn't like him. We battled, and it got to the point where it was just an intolerable working relationship. He was the senior partner. It wasn't up to him to leave; it was up to me to leave, so I did. I went to another firm in Jackson, a similar firm, and did defense work. These were some of the more traditional law firms in the city, and after a year or so in the second firm, I was just dissatisfied with working in a harness.

JD What advice would you give to lawyers or law students who want to start their own practice? What's the biggest mistake to avoid?

DS I think the biggest mistake to avoid is taking too many cases just to pay the rent. Use your judgment. Take some good cases, and even if you have to take bad cases, don't take more than a few. Work hard, don't spread yourself so thin that you can't focus, and be prepared for every case you take on.

JD Mississippi has many casinos. Are you a gambling man?

DS Maybe once a year, my wife and I play a little blackjack, but I never bet more than $100 or $200. I always lose.

STEPHEN BRIGHT
Interviewed in April 2002

Stephen Bright once told the *New York Times* that representing prisoners on death row was "brutal, enormously difficult, emotionally draining."

Bright's sober assessment of his practice went on: "There are no resources to do the job well, there's a tremendous amount of public hostility, and it's financially devastating to most lawyers. You have to be out of your head to take one of these cases." Crazy or not, Stephen Bright has been fighting to save death row inmates—and to oppose capital punishment—for more than two decades. Recently, death penalty issues have taken on new relevance. Al-Qaida or domestic terrorists may face capital trials. The execution of Timothy McVeigh, the first federally sanctioned killing in 38 years, focused renewed attention on the ultimate punishment. Likewise, DNA proof of wrongful convictions, capital cases involving the mentally retarded, issues of racial discrimination in the application of the death penalty, and questions about the quality of legal representation for death penalty defendants have all forced America to reconsider the wisdom of state-sponsored killing. As recently as eight years ago, 80 percent of Americans favored capital punishment; a recent ABC/*Washington Post* poll puts that number at 63 percent. As the death penalty debate reignites, Bright stands as the leading voice of the damned. The son of a Kentucky farmer, Bright graduated from the University of Kentucky College of Law in 1974 and cut his teeth as a trial attorney in the Washington, D.C., public defender's office. In 1979, he worked on a death penalty appeal for the American Civil Liberties Union, and three years later he signed on as director of the Southern Center for Human Rights (SCHR), a nonprofit law firm in Atlanta that represents disadvantaged inmates. Though he has moonlighted as a lecturer at Harvard, Yale, and Emory law schools, Bright's main focus is the SCHR, where he's written scholarly articles about the death penalty, won a key Supreme Court case regarding racial discrimination by jurors, and testified before Congress about death penalty issues. Bright recently spoke to *JD Jungle* about everything from the morality of the death penalty and the triumphs of his own career to his view of young lawyers and law students today. Crazy? You decide.

JD Jungle   Make the case against the death penalty.

Stephen Bright   It's morally wrong for people to kill, whether it's the state killing people or whether it's people killing each other. When the United States was a frontier society, we had few alternatives with regard to punishment. If somebody stole your horse, you could shoot them, you could hang them, you could put them in the stocks, you could whip them. Basically, we didn't have the prisons that we have today. And it's interesting that of all those rather primitive forms of punishment, the only one we still have is the death penalty. But even if one didn't have moral objections to the death penalty, consider the fact that so many people get death because of the poor quality of their court-appointed lawyer. Consider the fact that race plays such a role in who's sentenced to death. Or the fact that so many of those sentenced to death are mentally ill, some mentally retarded. Those factors, and the fact that we are surely killing innocent people— all of those are reasons we shouldn't have an irrevocable punishment.

JD   In 2000, Illinois governor George Ryan stopped executions in his state after evidence emerged of false convictions. George W. Bush, then the governor of Texas, said he was confident that all Texas death row inmates were guilty as charged. Your reaction?

SB Governor Bush—now President Bush—has no idea. I mean, he's been totally disengaged from the criminal justice process. He said that he spent 15 minutes to half an hour thinking about clemency or reprieves and the people who were executed—more than 150 people—over his six years as governor. George Bush has no more idea about the guilt or innocence of the people on death row than the average person reading this magazine does.

JD Lay out your strategy to oppose capital punishment.

SB My first hope is that other states will follow the lead of Governor Ryan and that we will see a moratorium declared while we look at this problem. Even some Texas legislators favor a moratorium bill. Second, we must reverse what has been a tremendous expansion of the death penalty over the past 20 years. If we are going to have the death penalty at all, it really should be restricted to the extraordinary cases—the "worst of the worst," as the courts say. Third is the effort to try to ensure that people get adequate legal representation. People should know that in Houston, Texas, for example, three people sentenced to death were represented by lawyers who slept through their capital trials, and that all three of those cases were later upheld on appeal by the Texas Court of Criminal Appeals. One of the men has since been executed. I doubt if George Bush knows that. But people should know that. That's simply not justice.

JD How do you plan to up the pressure politically?

SB I think the pressure is increasing just because of the concern that more and more people are having about the way in which the death penalty works in practice. DNA cases have gotten the attention of a lot of people in this country, and DNA has proven over and over and over again that the criminal justice system has convicted the wrong person. There's no reason to think that's happening any less in death penalty cases than it is in other cases. Quite to the contrary, the death penalty cases are usually tried with so much emotion. There's so much political gain on the part of the prosecutors and the judges caught up in those cases that there's actually a greater likelihood of mistakes.

JD In the ABC/*Washington Post* poll, support for capital punishment dropped below 50 percent when respondents considered an alternative sentence of life without parole. What do you make of that?

SB The death penalty has really been a result of the war on crime and the demagoguery and cynicism with regard to crime issues on the part of politicians. After [1988 presidential candidate Michael] Dukakis was so effectively beaten . . .

JD Flayed . . .

SB . . . yes, flayed with the Willie Horton ads. After that, then–governor [Bill] Clinton came back to Arkansas and made a spectacle of putting to death a brain-damaged person right before the New Hampshire primary in 1992. I think, unfortunately, the message that many politicians read out of that was: To show that you're tough on crime, you have to be for the death penalty. Not only do you have to be for the death penalty, you have to be for the death penalty in every conceivable crime.

JD What makes you think that politicians will ever roll back the death penalty?

SB Unfortunately, we live in a time when the politicians follow the people instead of leading them. What's needed is leadership on this issue—people who will talk sense about crime and punishment.

JD On a scale of 1 to 10, with 1 being not likely and 10 being 100 percent likely, how would you rate the odds of accomplishing your death penalty goals?

SB I don't know. Too much of the answer depends on things that are beyond our knowledge. We don't know, for example, when there will be a highly publicized case of an innocent person who's already been executed. I think what we have to do is be sort of like the people on the Underground Railroad, trying to get individuals across to safe passage one at a time by devoting our legal skills to that. At the same time, we have to raise these broader issues and hope that society will decide eventually to turn its back on this punishment.

JD Do you agree with those who said that televising Timothy McVeigh's execution would have spurred revulsion to the death penalty?

SB When we had public executions, which we had in this country up until the 1930s, they were carnivals. Now we have private executions, and very often they're carnivals, except that people don't get the voyeuristic pleasure of actually watching the execution. But my personal view is that it wouldn't have much effect. I think that this society has an interest in violence that is a bit unseemly. And if you look back at the pictures of people being lynched or look back at the public executions— like the one in Owensboro, Kentucky, where 20,000 people came—it's disturbing to see people there with their whole families. You've got Mom and Dad and the children, and they're all there smiling like they're at a picnic. Americans see so much death and violence on television and in the movies every day that we've become totally desensitized.

JD Why do so many Americans support the death penalty?

SB One of the reasons for the use of the death penalty has a lot to do with the sad state of race relations in the United States throughout our history. The death penalty is a direct descendent of slavery and racial oppression. When the South was getting bad press for lynching people in the '20s and '30s and '40s, the perfunctory death penalty trial became a way of accomplishing the same thing. You'd actually have cases where they would say, "Let the courts take care of it." The understood message was that the person would be given a quick trial, would be appointed some incompetent lawyer, and after a very perfunctory trial would soon be taken out back and hung or shot.

JD What do you say to victims' families and loved ones who say the death penalty brings them closure?

SB I'd defer to someone like Bud Welch, whose daughter was killed in the Oklahoma City bombing. He has pointed out that watching another human being put to death does not bring you closure. As one who has lost a loved one myself, I know that regardless of whether it's because of disease, crime, or accident, once someone is killed or dead, that person is never going to be restored. You're going to have that pain and that loss for the rest of your life. What's unfortunate is that the manipulation of victims of crime by politicians has resulted in people becoming obsessed with the legal cases involving the killers and not getting on with life.

JD You lost someone close to you?

SB My nephew, who was 18 years old, was killed in a car accident. When you've lost a member of your family, someone who was very close to you, there really is no such thing as closure. Closure is something you have in a real estate deal.

JD Sometimes you must know that your client is guilty of heinous crimes. How do you balance adhering to your moral beliefs with doing your job as a defense attorney?

SB I think that what a lawyer does is try to understand. Because it's never quite that simple. There's always a story. People are always much more than the worst thing they ever did in their life.

JD Do you try to focus on that?

SB In most of the death penalty cases that I have, the real issue is not guilt or innocence, the issue is punishment. The person is going to be found guilty of capital murder. The question is, are they going to be punished with the death penalty, or with life in prison, or with life in prison without parole? My focus is on who is this person, what is their life and background, how did they get to this place in life that they committed this heinous crime? And how can I convince a jury—while acknowledging my client's responsibility for the crime—that this person will be punished severely and the community will be protected by a sentence of life in prison?

JD What led you to practice human rights law?

SB I had the good fortune to grow up in the '60s, when there was a lot of concern about civil rights, about human rights, about equality, and about making good on promises that are in our Constitution and in our Declaration of Independence that have never been realized. It seemed to me then, and it still seems to me today, that trying to realize those aspirations of equal justice—not discriminating, treating people fairly—is very much worthwhile.

JD Did you have legal heroes?

SB Thurgood Marshall is one. Also, Clarence Darrow and Bill Kunstler. Then there's my first boss, who's not as well known but who's a great, great lawyer: John Rosenberg, the former director of the Appalachian Research and Defense Fund of Kentucky, who spent more than 30 years in the coalfields of Appalachia providing the highest quality legal representation to poor people.

JD Some lawyers argue that pro bono should be mandated. Where do you stand?

SB I think it's more important that we adequately fund public-defender programs and legal-services programs so that poor people are provided with access to the legal system. That is never going to be accomplished by pro bono representation. The quality of legal representation provided to most poor people accused of crimes in this country, whether it's murder or shoplifting, is a scandal. Any system that wants to claim that it provides equal justice under law cannot continue the way ours is going now. We're going to have to either sandblast that phrase off the Supreme Court building or adequately fund legal programs to provide legal services to poor people in criminal cases. That will never be accomplished by pro bono efforts.

JD So you oppose mandating pro bono service?

SB My only worry about mandatory pro bono is that the people will do the work grudgingly and not enthusiastically. I suppose, on balance, it's probably better to have it done even that way, because it will at least expose people to the problems. One of the things that is a tremendous problem in the legal profession today is that lawyers live in expensive homes, drive in fancy automobiles, park in their private parking places, and work in their mahogany offices, and they never see the poor people. They never see the mentally ill people on the streets going through the garbage cans trying to find a little food to eat. And they simply don't realize how there are people who are up against it in our society. I think it's very important that lawyers be exposed to that, but I'm not as convinced as a lot of people are that we're going to do much of that through pro bono.

JD Why should a law student forgo a six-figure salary for a career in human rights law?

SB Human rights law is lucrative in terms of the fulfillment. Many people in law firms are making a lot of money but aren't very happy about what they're doing. Many people don't realize until it's too late that it's better to do something and get nothing for it than to do nothing and get something for it.

JD Did you ever go on any interviews for, or pursue, a more typical mainstream legal career?

SB I never had any interest in working for a law firm. I never interviewed with one. I never sent a resumé to one.

JD You've been quoted as saying, "The challenge in law school is to keep the fire burning." What did you mean?

SB I think if you wanted to invent an institution that would take young, idealistic, smart people, who have some commitment to the public interest, and turn them into supporters of the establishment, you really cannot improve upon the modern American law school.

JD Then law schools are to blame for producing selfish young lawyers?

SB The law schools bear some responsibility, and the law firms bear some, too. The fact is, if you offer someone

$130,000 to do something, versus $30,000, most people in our society are going to take the $130,000. Law schools are responsible for high tuitions and a lack of loan-forgiveness programs, which are absolutely essential if we're going to have public-interest programs. I also think students have to take some responsibility for their own lives. A lot of law students are risk-avoidance people; they're in law school because they haven't really decided what they want to do with their lives. And instead of deciding, they sort of get pulled along in the stream.

JD What's your single proudest achievement as a lawyer?

SB Probably the day that I watched Tony Amadeo, who had been sentenced to death in Georgia when he was 18 years old, graduate summa cum laude from Mercer University while he was still in prison. I was one of a team of people who represented him; I argued his case before the Supreme Court.

JD And your most disillusioning day as a lawyer?

SB If you're in the practice I'm in, there are many disillusioning days.

JD But tell me about your worst day.

SB Perhaps the most disillusioning was the day that *McCleskey* v. *Kemp* came down. When the Supreme Court said that, despite the patterns of racial discrimination, the death penalty in Georgia could still be carried out. I remember being with a number of civil rights leaders in Atlanta that day, and many of them were crying. Just the notion that the Court would say, as it did in *McCleskey*, that these racial disparities are inevitable was extremely disheartening.

JD Give the current Supreme Court a letter grade.

SB One of the problems with the Supreme Court today is that none of them know what it's like to be up against it. That's unfortunate. If you read some of the tributes that were written to Justice Marshall when he died, one of the things that he gave the Court was a tie to reality. If the Court were in touch with the reality of life in America today, they would not say that it's reasonable to arrest someone and take him to jail for not wearing a seat belt.

JD Their grade?

SB D.

JD Some people refer to you as "the Saint."

SB That's totally inappropriate. I have had the tremendous privilege of being able to spend almost every day of my practice doing things I care about and believe in. I think one of the things we lose sight of is just how privileged we are in this profession.

JD So what's the single most important piece of advice you can give a young lawyer today?

SB Don't sell out.

VERNON JORDAN
Interviewed in March 2002

After his sophomore year at Indiana's DePauw University, Vernon Jordan Jr. had planned to spend the summer of 1955 in Atlanta, his hometown, interning at the Continental Insurance Company. Jordan believed that the recruiter's promise of a position was as solid as one of the firm's insurance policies, but on the day he turned up for work, the director of the summer program called him into his office.

"They did not tell us," the man said.

"They did not tell you what?" Jordan asked.

"They did not tell us you were colored."

Jordan's job offer was withdrawn.

Such a snub might have crushed a less determined man, but it only inspired Jordan, who's repeatedly shrugged off prejudice—and more—to become one of the most powerful business, legal, and political figures in America.

After graduating from DePauw and Howard University School of Law, Jordan fought on the front lines of the war for civil rights. In 1961, just a year out of Howard, the 25-year-old lawyer was tapped by the NAACP to be its Georgia field director. A decade later, Jordan was running the National Urban League. During the 1970s, politicians vying for black votes sought Jordan's stamp of approval, as did companies striving to integrate their boardrooms. Despite fierce criticism from colleagues who frowned on the idea of civil rights leaders working for big business, Jordan joined the boards of several major corporations, including Xerox and Bankers Trust, while continuing to work at the Urban League.

On May 29, 1980, Jordan traveled to Fort Wayne, Indiana, for the Urban League's annual Equal Opportunity Dinner. After the event, Jordan was invited to the home of Urban League member Martha Coleman, a white woman, for coffee. Coleman had just dropped off Jordan at his hotel when a sniper fired a bullet into his back, nearly severing his spine. Only after five operations and 16 days was it clear that Jordan would survive. "I was shot because I was black and in the company of a white woman," Jordan writes in his 2001 memoir *Vernon Can Read!* (PublicAffairs). The accused gunman, a white supremacist named Joseph Paul Franklin, was later convicted of unrelated race-based crimes.

In 1982, Jordan left the Urban League to take a partnership at the Washington office of the law firm Akin, Gump, Strauss, Hauer & Feld. He prospered there and became one of Washington's most influential power brokers, especially after his friend and golf partner Bill Clinton was elected to the White House in 1992. Jordan made headlines for his role in the Monica Lewinsky scandal (when Lewinsky left a Pentagon job in 1997, Jordan, a Revlon board director, helped her get a job offer with the firm), but he emerged from the incident relatively unscathed. In 2000, Jordan joined Lazard, the international investment bank, as a senior managing director, adding a new line to his platinum-plated resumé.

Jordan spoke with *JD Jungle* at his Lazard office in New York. The man who was once turned away from an internship at the Continental Insurance Company because he was "colored" talked about his diverse career and about diversity in the workplace, then and now.

JD JUNGLE   Do you think people of color see more or less opportunity ahead of them than you saw when you were growing up?

VERNON JORDAN   There's no question they see more. I spoke the other day to the black alumni of Harvard Business School. When I first came to New York in 1970, we could have had that meeting in a phone booth. And I'm looking there at a whole roomful of young, talented black MBAs who are all on Wall Street—and Main Street. When I was growing up, and when I came out of law school in 1960, there were all sorts of limitations on what I could do. I couldn't even take the bar review course, let alone work for the government as a lawyer. And the notion that you would be in a law firm was just unbelievable. Now virtually all jobs in law and business are available to young black men and women.

JD   What limitations do minorities entering law or business still face today?

VJ   The numbers still aren't what they ought to be. Specific percentages I don't have, but I know that it's not enough.

JD   Why do you think that is?

VJ   It's historic. It's the failure of law firms and investment banks to commit to the effort. Where institutions in corporate America have, in fact, committed, you see the results. And where there is no commitment, the results are bad. I do not attribute it to racism as much as I attribute it to lack of effort. There's a lot of lip service. And in difficult times, as we're going through now, people tend not to focus so much on diversity, because they're focused on survival. That's a mistake.

JD   Suppose you were diversity czar. What steps should the federal government, law firms, and corporations take to increase the numbers?

VJ   Every company, every boardroom in which I sit has a plan, and each has objectives, goals, and a process. And to make it work, the pressure and incentive have to come from the top. A lot of companies make diversity a part of the performance goals against which an executive gets paid. Just as you have to make a certain sales number, you have to make a diversity number to get your bonus. That is more difficult to do in a law firm, but there are ways to do it. I am for as much pressure as can be put. I also think the initiative for that pressure has to be sustained by civil rights organizations, and at some points you have got to take people to court. The fight is still worth fighting.

JD   What role should the federal government play?

VJ   They could be more aggressive. They could stop talking about this being a "color-blind" society. That's nonsense. This is not a color-blind society. They could be more aggressive at the EEOC [Equal Employment Opportunity Commission] and at the OFCCP [Office of Federal Contract Compliance Programs].

JD   Have your feelings about affirmative action changed since the '50s?

VJ   I was for it then, and I'm for it now. I haven't changed on that one bit. And if need be, I'm for quotas. I'm old-fashioned. If there are no black people—get some.

JD   Do minorities have a special obligation to help other minorities get ahead?

VJ   I'm here because I stand on many, many shoulders, and that's true of every black person I know who has achieved. We understand that we did not get where we are by ourselves, and we understand that we have to pass that on to young people—that's why I went to talk to the Harvard Business School black alumni. At the same time, there's a reality. You're a banker or lawyer, you're just starting out, and you really want to give back. But you're working 70- and 80-hour weeks, so it's difficult. But there will come a time and a place to give back, and each individual will recognize that time and place. For the most part, they do just that.

JD   Make the case for diversifying the workplace.

VJ   We are America. We have a Fourteenth Amendment that talks about equal protection of the laws. We are a government of, by, and for the people. The law says we shall not discriminate based on race, sex, sexual orientation. So the case is easy.

JD   Do you expect that September 11, which has brought Americans together in many ways, might aid the cause of diversity?

VJ   I think September 11 stands on its own as a terrible tragedy. But tragedy tends to blur what's historically clear.

Terrorism is not new to black people. We've always known terrorism: the lynchings in the South; the four little girls at Birmingham; Medgar, Martin, and Malcolm. So we know a little bit more about terrorism from our own brothers and sisters—white people. As I watched the national prayer service at the National Cathedral, it dawned on me that there was no National Day of Prayer for the four little girls at Birmingham. Now, given time and progress, there probably would be. When the Oklahoma City bombing took place, because it was an integrated federal building, you had to mourn everybody; and because the World Trade Center towers were in fact integrated, you could not do what they did to black veterans when they came back from Vietnam—to try to bury them in separate cemeteries. So we've made a lot of progress.

JD When will we know that full equality has been achieved in the workplace?

VJ I don't know the answer to that, and if anybody tells you that they know the answer to that, don't count on it.

JD Do you think it will be in your lifetime?

VJ I hope.

Appendix A

Resource List

www.abanet.org
Website for the American Bar Association

www.lsac.org
Your gateway to the Law School Admission Council

www.nalp.org
National Association for Law Placement

www.napil.org
Equal Justice Works (formerly National
Association for Public Interest Law)

www.usnews.com/usnews/edu/grad/rankings/law/lawindex.htm
This year's rankings of the country's top law schools

www.ncbl.org
The National Conference of Black Lawyers

www.hnba.com
The Hispanic National Bar Association

www.nativeamericanbar.org
The National Native American Bar Association

www.napaba.org
The National Asian Pacific American Bar Association

Appendix B

....

Top Law Schools

Source: *U.S. News & World Report* rankings, 2003

1. Yale University (CT)
2. Stanford University (CA)
3. Harvard University (MA)
4. Columbia University (NY)
5. New York University
6. University of Chicago
7. University of California–Berkeley
   University of Michigan–Ann Arbor
   University of Pennsylvania
   University of Virginia
11. Northwestern University (IL)
12. Duke University (NC)
13. Cornell University (NY)
14. Georgetown University (DC)
15. University of Texas–Austin
16. University of California–Los Angeles
17. Vanderbilt University (TN)
18. University of Iowa

University of Minnesota–Twin Cities
University of Southern California
Washington and Lee University (VA)
22. Boston College
    Emory University (GA)
24. University of Notre Dame (IN)
25. Boston University
    George Washington University (DC)
    University of Illinois–Urbana-Champaign
    University of Washington
    University of Wisconsin–Madison
    Washington University in St. Louis
31. University of North Carolina–Chapel Hill
32. College of William and Mary (VA)
    Fordham University (NY)
    University of California–Davis
    University of Georgia
36. Wake Forest University (NC)
37. Brigham Young University (J. Reuben Clark) (UT)
    Ohio State University (Moritz)
39. Indiana University–Bloomington
40. University of Arizona
    University of California (Hastings)
    University of Colorado–Boulder
43. Tulane University (LA)
    University of Connecticut
45. University of Florida (Levin)
    University of Utah (S.J. Quinney)
47. George Mason University (VA)
    University of Alabama
49. American University (Washington College of Law)
        (DC)
    Southern Methodist University (TX)
    University of Kentucky

Contributors

Maurice Black
David Blend
James Burnett
Krysten Crawford
Lorraine Dusky
Susan Estrich
Jack Hitt
Nina Johnson
Dimitra Kessenides
Mark Murray
Erin O'Connor
Alexis Offen
Kristen Olson
Ted Rose
Randi Rothberg
Sascha Segan
Hanna Stotland
David Wallis
L. Adrienne Wichard

Jungle Media Group would also like to thank the following people for their work on this book:
Rebecca Geiger
Roland Lange

John Kline
Anna Moschovakis
Sara Tucker
Rena Pacella

Note: Some portions of this book that have appeared in *JD Jungle* or on jdjungle.com have been modified or updated since their original publication.

Index

JUNGLE MEDIA GROUP

CO-FOUNDERS

Jon Housman, Jonathan McBride, Sean McDuffy

ADVISORY BOARD

John Berg, Jeff Bernstein, James M. Borth, George Daly, Elie Housman, Kevin O'Malley, Julius Sarkozy

MANY THANKS TO

Steven Audi, Jeff Bernstein, Seth Bogner, W. Stewart Cahn, Peter Cohen, Greg Coleman, Peter Dunn, Roysi Erbes, Robyn Fruchterman, Phillip Getter, Godfrey Gill, Robert Gold, Rosalie Goldberg, Jay Hachigian, Richard Hesp, Sean Kelly, Ken Koch, Jennifer Lemaigre, Al Lieberman, Gregory Miller, Susan Miller, Faris Naber, Randy Rock, Whitney Tilson, Steven Weinstein, Lawrence J. Weissman

Jungle Media Group
632 Broadway, 7th Floor
New York, NY 10012
Phone: 866-4JUNGLE
Fax: 212-352-9282
www.junglemediagroup.com

JD Jungle and *MBA Jungle* subscriptions (8 issues):
U.S. $24.97
Canada $33.97
International $46.97
For queries and customer service, call 866-251-0840 or go to www.junglemediagroup.com

ABOUT JUNGLE MEDIA GROUP

Jungle Media Group is the recognized authority for reaching the new generation of leaders.

The company's mission is to inform, entertain, and provide its audience with the tools they need to master the art of success. Jungle's properties include *JD Jungle* and *MBA Jungle* magazines, and the websites jdjungle.com and mbajungle.com. The company was founded by Jon Housman, Jonathan McBride, and Sean McDuffy. Jon Housman is an adjunct professor at the NYU–Stern School of Business. He was previously a consultant with McKinsey & Company. Jonathan McBride is a graduate of the Wharton Business School who previously worked as an associate at Goldman Sachs, and he currently serves on the board of trustees of Connecticut College. Sean McDuffy, also a Wharton graduate, is an alumnus of both McKinsey & Company and Goldman Sachs.